My Life
in the
Middle
Ages

My Life
in the
Middle
Ages

❖ A Survivor's Tale ❖

James Atlas

HarperCollins*Publishers*

HarperCollins books may be purchased for educational, business, or sales promotional use. For information, please write: Special Markets Department, HarperCollins Publishers Inc., 10 East 53rd Street, New York, NY 10022.

FIRST EDITION

Designed by Nancy Singer Olaguera

Printed on acid-free paper

Library of Congress Cataloging-in-Publication Data is available upon request.

ISBN 0-06-019629-7

05 06 07 08 09 ❖ /RRD   10 9 8 7 6 5 4 3 2 1

For Anna, Molly, and William

Contents

Introduction   ix

Mom and Dad   1

Time   35

Home   49

Money   65

Failure   87

Shrinks   110

The Body   132

Books   148

God   165

Twenty-fifth Anniversary   195

Death   208

Acknowledgments   219

Introduction

This is a book that came about by accident.

In 1996, Tina Brown offered me a job as a staff writer at *The New Yorker*. I was no more immune than any other writer in America to *The New Yorker*'s immense cultural power, but there was something about the magazine that had always troubled me: the "Talk of the Town" voice, with its coy, anonymous use of "we," or the interminable articles on obscure subjects. Then there was the self-absorption of the *New Yorker*'s staff, whose sprightly memoirs about life at the magazine and the foibles of its eccentric stable of pampered writers made the place seem like a grown-up version of my high school cafeteria, rife with cliques and factions and a "cool crowd." I pretended that I had no wish to join it, and probably couldn't have in any case. I had grown up in a suburb of Chicago and, despite decades of living in the East, had never felt entirely comfortable with its sophisticated style.

Tina's *New Yorker* was more inclusive. She refused to be intimidated by the magazine's hoary traditions. If she didn't feel like putting its monocled mascot, Eustace Tilley, on the cover once a year, she didn't; she fired the magazine's nonproducing legends, writers who hadn't written anything in years, even decades, yet who continued to occupy offices. Tasked with preserving the old traditions while renovating a publication whose fustian tone rendered it a media-world museum piece, she had the temerity to put in photographs, contributors' notes, and bylines for "Talk of the Town." No wonder people resented Tina. She was tampering with an icon. There were other reasons, too, notably her bent for provocation and her insatiable appetite for "buzz"—a Tina coinage for gossip. Whatever the precise reasons for the passions she stirred up, the brief era over which she presided was as revolutionary in the magazine world as Cromwell's revolt against Charles I.

Four years into her tenure at the magazine, Tina called and asked me to write a piece on "the death of fun." The thesis, apparently concocted at an "ideas" meeting, was that everyone—at least in Tina's world—worked too hard these days; no one ever just went out on the town and had a good time. I had been chosen for this assignment, it emerged, on the grounds that I was reputed to be one of the few people around who still *did* manage to have fun once in a while. I was baffled by this wild surmise; I was hardly a partygoer and spent the majority of my nights hunched over a book or with my children, watching baboons display their rumps on *Nature*. But what Tina had in mind was pretty clear: we lived in a money culture now, squeezed by downsizing, tied to the wheel of ambition. The drunken dinner party, the joint inhaled in a taxi full of revelers careening through SoHo at dawn—these were scenes out of ancient history, I suggested in my piece, exotica recorded in some yellowed Jay McInerney novel already gathering dust on the shelf. If I had to come up with a symbolic representation of the prevailing ethos, it would be a series of red circles, each with a line through it: No Smoking, No Drinking, No Sex. No Fun.

The piece touched a nerve. For weeks afterward, fat packets of letters were forwarded almost daily from the magazine, registering a wide and vociferous range of opinion—so many that the mail room printed up my own private address label. I was shaken by the decibel-level of virulence. Aging swingers and aggressively offbeat characters proud of their dissolute ways thought I was a prig. "Get a grip!" one advised. "Piss out a high-story window!" remonstrated a Brooklyn freelancer (who, once he'd vented, offered to buy me dinner at an all-night Polish diner in the East Village). But there were also many readers who identified with the pathos of my theme and grasped what I was getting at: every generation is forced to endure its own obsolescence. The world was more fun when we were young because we thought we owned it. "The tragedy of old age is not that one is old, but that one is young," wrote Oscar Wilde. Yet nothing can prepare us for what it feels like to be ushered out. Each generation regards with incredulity the prospect of its own mortality. In the shadow of my lighthearted piece a somber message lurked.

Suspecting that she was on to something—a hunger among people of a certain age and social standing to read about themselves—Tina proposed another piece, on the crazy, status-obsessed culture of New York private schools. Our daughters attended the same Upper East Side school—I used to see her stepping into her Town Car mornings after she had dropped her daughter off at school. I recorded amazing stories I'd heard, satirized the child-obsession of Manhattanites, the competitive drawing exercises of nursery-school kids facing the admissions process, the SAT-tutoring fetish.

I was beginning to get the hang of it: write about your own experience as a way of writing about your generation. I wrote a piece on failure that chronicled some of my own literary ups and downs over the years—most notably the failure of a novel I'd published in my late thirties. Once again, the piece struck a nerve. I was deluged with confessional mail: "My husband's downsizing . . ." "During my bankruptcies . . ." "It's a cold winter day and I'm wasting another day at the Chicago Board of Trade, bored to death . . ." "I spent a year in my house in Malibu sitting in a chair and staring at the wall." I felt like Miss Lonelyhearts, inadvertently tapping into the fathomless pool of human pain, regret, humiliation, sorrow, misfortune, disaster, and tragedy buried under the cheerful surface of most lives. "I am thirty-six, separated and very much rudderless right now . . ." "I'm fifty-two. My parents were divorced when I was thirteen . . ." (This letter was accompanied by photographs of the author's wife in the nude.) "At forty-one and three-quarters, I quit my job at CBS to pursue my dream of making films . . ." "I've been trying to write fiction off and on all my life, and I'm now in my seventy-fifth year . . ." (I'll be happy if I get that far.)

Two more pieces followed, on my family and on the meaning of money. Published under the various headings "Domestic Life," "Personal History," and "Department of Stocktaking," these "personal pieces"—as I came to think of them—explored the predicaments my cohort faced as their children grew up and their parents grew old. Caught in the middle, we constituted what sociologists refer to as "the Sandwich Generation"—not an easy position to navigate with grace. The piece on money was harder to write and elicited annoyance in some quarters. Money is a charged issue—more charged, it's often said, than sex—and to write about it honestly is to risk offending those who don't have enough, those who don't feel they have enough, and those who have enough but don't have the sense to know it. I ventured to name actual sums—probably a mistake. Honesty, I was beginning to discover, may not always be the best policy.

A year after I arrived at the magazine, Tina left (to start the short-lived *Talk*). A new editor—David Remnick—arrived, with his own interests and preoccupations. But there was more to say on the subject. In conversation, in the books I read, in articles about my social class and type, I kept encountering themes that resonated, above all the dawning recognition that we were on the verge of reaching our limits—of middle age, of our physical and mental capacities, of what life in our remaining years could offer. It wasn't over, but we had embarked on the home stretch. My father had an image for it: at his fiftieth birthday party, he announced to his assembled friends that he was now on the downward slope of the bell curve. At fifty, you could just make out the far horizon and what lay beyond it—"Twilight and evening bell, and after that the dark." The moment of coming to terms was at hand.

Virtually nothing is left in this book of the articles I wrote for *The New Yorker*. It's not a collection of pieces; it's not a memoir. Those looking for confession and brutal self-disclosure will do better to look elsewhere. The eleven chapters are intended to create a unity: it's deliberate that each opens in the same way. What I've tried to write could be called, perhaps, a generational memoir. The one legacy of the pieces I wrote for *The New Yorker* is the voice they helped me find.

I realize that, on one level, these pieces describe only a highly rarefied segment of society: the middle- and upper-middle-class Manhattan dwellers who lead lives of privilege. I write about people with interesting jobs that pay well; families, children, nice homes or apartments; vacations, disposable income; therapy if they need it (or think they need it); and a far larger share of happiness, however elusive and hard-won, than most people in the world enjoy. But it's also my hope that readers beyond the city limits will recognize themselves in these pages.

I'm aware of my good luck. If the tone of these essays is on occasion sad or regretful, it rarely descends to darkness. But does the fact that I've suffered no great tragedy mean that I've gone through life unscathed? Even the lucky ones experience pain, loss, and disappointment. The greatest challenge of middle age, it seems to me—and as I write these words, I'm on the threshold of late middle age, which imposes a biological deadline far more terrifying than the demands of any editor—is to accept one's limitations. It's not easy. In my experience, it's the hardest thing of all.

My Life
in the
Middle
Ages

Mom and Dad

"**D**ad's in the hospital."

So it begins.

I'm in the kitchen of our summer house in Vermont when I get the call from my mother. It's a Saturday morning in early June, and birds are peeping in the tangle of greenery outside the window. I can hear the whine of my neighbor's Weed Eater as he trims underbrush across the road. "Dad" is my dad, not hers, but at this point, after sixty-four years of marriage, they've become so inextricable, bound together in so many complex ways, that the terms *husband* and *wife* no longer adequately describe their relationship. They are also each other's children, now that my brother and I have moved away; and parents, their own having been in the ground for decades. They are no longer, I assume, lovers, at least not in the technical sense: my father is eighty-seven, my mother eighty-three. But who knows? They're a family unto themselves—a family of two. Hence *Dad*. He in turn addresses her as *Mother*.

"What's the matter?"

She launches into a breathlessly detailed account (she jokingly refers to herself as "the long-winded lady," after the garrulous correspondent who filed occasional columns for *The New Yorker*'s "Talk of the Town" many years ago, when the section was still unsigned) of how he woke up the day before and couldn't move his arm, and the house doctor at Brookhaven, the assisted-living facility in Lexington, Massachusetts, to which they moved seven months ago, came to look at it and couldn't figure out what was going on and called an ambulance that took him to the emergency room of Beth Israel Hospital in Boston "where we had to wait *seven hours* for them to do a CAT scan of his brain . . ."

"Why his brain?" I've only been half-listening up to this point, preoccupied watching a scarlet tanager hop back and forth on a branch. My father had a minor stroke a decade ago, which caused him to lose some movement in his right hand—no more playing the oboe or the piano, his favorite pastimes. Otherwise he'd been in perfect health. A small trim man, he had a light tan in all weather, and skin as smooth as a peach. He didn't have the dusty, crinkled look, the stooped gait and curved spine of what I thought of as the "old old." He'd only given up tennis a year or two ago—"picking up balls," he'd taken to calling it near the end. He never allowed himself to go around looking decrepit and had a walk-in closet stocked (mostly by his tireless shopper of a wife) with crisply ironed shirts, tweed jackets, soft leather lace-up shoes polished to a high sheen. In a hanging closet bag were linen suits from Bullocks Wilshire in La Jolla, California, where he and my mother had lived for thirty years after he retired from his medical practice in Chicago at the youthful age of fifty-seven.

His fitness didn't stop him from predicting his own imminent demise. He was surprisingly pessimistic about his chances in the death lottery, even after he'd outlived so many of his friends. My father's method of warding off senescence was to act as if it had already arrived. *You can't fire me: I quit.* "How many years have I got left?" he would say; or, "I won't be around much longer"—meanwhile struggling to master the Internet as he sat crouched in front of his new iMac as intently as an air controller navigating traffic at LaGuardia. From a statistical and biological perspective, he was nearing the end of his span; his walk had slowed and he had trouble hearing. His eyesight was beginning to fail. "At our age, you can go down like this," he would say, plunging his liver-spotted hands earthward in a dive-bomb gesture. But he could still get around on his own and joked in a good-natured way about the residents of Brookhaven, referring to them as "old people." Whenever he passed one of his neighbors shuffling down the corridor with a walker, he picked up his pace, eager to differentiate himself. Flattening himself against a wall as an elderly lady in a wide-brimmed hat whizzed by in a motorized cart, he joked, "It's like the Indianapolis Five Hundred around here."

Their traveling days were over. In their seventies my parents had gone to Cambodia and China, to Europe and Israel. They always came east to visit us at Thanksgiving, braving the throngs in Times Square to take the grandchildren to a Broadway show. But they weren't entirely housebound even now. Three months after they sold their house and moved to the Boston suburbs to be near my brother, they had gone back to La Jolla for a month, arranging for a comfortable sublet with a view of the ocean. My persistent mother had wangled an upgrade of their frequent-flier miles. "I could get used to first class," she bragged. No, it wasn't time; it wasn't over. "I'm old, dear," she would remind me in a feeble, apologetic voice if I got short-tempered on the phone. ("No, Mom: we're picking him up at hockey camp, *then* we're dropping her off at riding camp." What are you, senile?) "I know you don't like to talk about this," she had told me firmly a few months before, describing her busy efforts to divest herself of possessions. She was sorting through the clumps of family photographs stuffed in drawers and pasting them in albums or tossing them out; she had located their life insurance policy;

she had put up for sale at a local auction house the collection of ivory figurines collected over the years. What was their hurry?

Holding the phone to my ear, I detect in my mother's voice an uncharacteristic note of urgency. "They still don't know what it is," she says. "They're doing more tests. It could be . . ." She falls silent.

"What, Mom?"

"I don't know."

It's Anna, my wife the doctor, who gently introduces the term after I summarize what I've been told: "A carcinoma of the brain?" Even then, I'm calm, able to shake off the stitch of anxiety that grips my chest. Somehow the word *carcinoma* is less frightening than *cancer*—more clinical, more detached. But the possibility has at last been introduced. I sit on the steps of our house and look out at the field. A hawk circles overhead. For some reason, I feel weirdly at peace.

Two days later, I'm striding down the hall of the intensive care unit at Boston's Beth Israel Hospital, on the way to my father's room. At the nurses' station, doctors and residents are scribbling their notes or talking on the phone; green-smocked orderlies hustle up and down the stretcher-clogged halls with trays of food. I glance through the open doors of rooms and see patients stretched out on their beds, watching TV or dozing or just lying there comatose, mouths open in what medical personnel refer to as "the O sign."

My father is upright in bed, with his glasses off. His head looks tiny on the pillow. Wordlessly, he embraces me. His body feels light and papery, as if it could float off into space. My mother rises from her chair, and I lean down to give her a kiss on the cheek. She, too, feels frail. She's never been robust and suffers from a variety of ailments—crushing migraines, skin cancer, heart fibrillations—but she's never been really sick either. My parents have devoted the last three decades to preserving themselves; they enjoyed their lives—their daily walks, their dinners out, their holidays with the family. They weren't ready to say good-bye without putting up some resistance. To this end, they found an environment—Southern California—in which the weather was perfect; they lived low-stress lives, puttering about their Japanese garden amid the bonsai trees my father loved to tend; they took long walks in their sturdy pastel-colored sneakers on the nearby campus of the University of California; they were obsessively vigilant about their diets, removing the skin from chicken with surgical precision, reducing salt and butter intake, maintaining what my father liked to call "a thin edge of hunger." Only now, after decades of being held at bay, put off, delayed, filibustered by their fanatical adherence to the nutritional theories of Dr. Dean Ornish, is mortality beginning to gain the upper hand.

"So, Sonny," my father says wanly. "What brings you here?" As if I had just wandered in by chance, unannounced and unexpected. As if my arrival weren't a portent but a happy coincidence.

"Just checking up on you," I say.

How fast it's happened. Could it have been only thirty years—twenty-eight, actually, I calculate—since I accompanied my father to the Hebrew nursing home on the North Side of Chicago where his mother sat uncomprehending in a wheelchair, her eyes milky and clouded, white hairs sprouting from her chin, and listened to him chatter as he bustled purposefully about the barren room? "Hello, Mother! How are you? How do you feel?" And now it was my turn. Thirty years: a generation.

Lying on his hospital bed, my father reminds me of a medieval king I once saw carved in wood on a coffin in some ancient Cotswold church. How small men were back then! Their bodies were stunted by poor nutrition and disease. My son at thirteen, a giant with sturdy milk-fed bones, towers over me. I hope I live to see *his* son; he'll probably have the body mass of Samson.

"How do you feel?" I ask.

"I'm okay," he says in a feeble voice. "I wish they knew what was wrong."

All afternoon doctors arrive and brief us, a parade of specialists accompanied by clusters of interns and residents, nurses taking my father's temperature and his blood pressure, orderlies cranking his bed up and down. A battery of tests and X-rays and scans has failed to reveal what's wrong with him. The two most likely possibilities are a brain abscess or a tumor, but it could be something else—another stroke, or cancer originating in a different organ that's metastasized and affected his brain.

Despite the literal death-threat hanging over him, he's enjoying the attention. "I've got 'em stumped," he crows. Dusting off his medical expertise—"I started out as a neurologist," he informs every doctor who appears in the doorway—he diagnoses his own symptoms. "I'd rule out a stroke, since there's no impairment of speech; it could be a localized benign tumor." Whatever it is, it's causing a stir. My father's illness has become a special case.

My mother is outwardly calm, knitting in her chair. My brother, Steve, a producer of TV documentaries, is in Uzbekistan on assignment. His wife, my sister-in-law, Robin, has been trying to track him down. Finally he calls me on my cell phone. "Where are you?" I ask. "I'm in a yurt," he says, "lying on a mattress stuffed with straw. There's a yak just outside my window. I guess that's what it is: I've never seen a yak before." We both laugh and then, just as suddenly, begin to cry. I don't know if it's because he's so far away, his voice coming to me from somewhere on the far side of the globe, or the emergency nature of the whole event—the tiny Motorola StarTAC held to my ear; the disembodied voice of my only sibling, twelve thousand miles away, making contact with me in a hospital room as nurses hurry in and out—but our tearful laughter brings home the reality of what's happening: our father is gravely ill. Steve promises to get a flight out as soon as he can. He'll be home in two days.

By nine o'clock that night, the surgeon who was supposed to come and examine my father still hasn't shown up. My father has gotten it into his head that he definitely has a tumor, and that they're going to wheel him off in the morning, lay him out on the operating table, and remove it. I decide to stay overnight in his room, and the nurses bring in a cot for me. My mother doesn't want to leave, but after my father has had his dinner—orange Jell-O, a slice of turkey with mashed potatoes and gravy, a plastic bowl of rice pudding—I persuade her to go home in a taxi and then crawl under the blanket on my narrow bed.

Unable to sleep, I listen to the hiss and sigh of oxygen tanks, the stertorous groans of the man across the hall, who keeps summoning a nurse and begging her to up his morphine dose. From other rooms come the beeping sounds, like a forklift truck backing up, of various machines. The floor has the high-alert atmosphere of a NASA control room: heart monitors; EKG machines with their stuttering lines squiggling across a graph; tangled tube coils attached to intravenous drips.

My father can't sleep either. The doctors refused to give him a sedative, explaining that it would interfere with the tests they've been doing on his brain. "I feel like I'm being swept out to sea," he says—a haunting image. To distract himself, he recites over and over the first stanza of Yeats's "The Second Coming" in a hoarse voice. My mother confided to me that he had been disappearing into the bathroom in the middle of the night lately, and she couldn't figure out what he was doing in there. One day she found in a drawer a sheet of yellow lined paper on which he'd copied out the lines of Yeats's poem. He was memorizing it. In the night, he mutters:

> Turning and turning in the widening gyre
> The falcon cannot hear the falconer;
> Things fall apart; the centre cannot hold;
> Mere anarchy is loosed upon the world,

The blood-dimmed tide is loosed, and everywhere
The ceremony of innocence is drowned;
The best lack all conviction, while the worst
Are full of passionate intensity.

My father is a bookish man. Our home was filled with books: *Ulysses* and *Finnegans Wake*, Edith Hamilton's *Greek Mythology*, Hannah Arendt's *The Human Condition*, William Barrett's *Irrational Man*. He loves to read aloud. I grew up listening to the classics. We would settle down in the living room with our books after dinner, my mother rustling the *Sun-Times*, my father in his black leather Herman Miller chair, a heavy volume on his lap. "Listen to this," he would say, sharing a favorite passage until, enacting a family joke, I'd slip off the couch and crawl from the room while my father droned on obliviously about the misadventures of Leopold Bloom. Whenever someone asked if I had read *Ulysses*, I'd reply, "No, but I heard it."

In the hospital room, we lie side by side in our beds like two boys in a cabin at summer camp. My father tells me things about his life I'd never known: how his father, Herman, an immigrant Jew from Poland who had managed to earn an engineering degree from a university in Moscow despite the prohibition against Jews living in cities, came to America at the turn of the century and worked in the steel mills of Detroit and Kansas City. Eventually he got laid off. Not long after my father was born, the family moved to Valparaiso, Indiana, where Herman enrolled in pharmacy school. In Russia, he had acquired what my father enjoyed describing as "a superior European education." He could speak and read five languages; he was conversant with the Great Books—or at least with the compressed versions that every immigrant had on his shelf, the Haldeman-Julius blue books. But he still needed to support his family. When my father was twelve, they migrated to

Chicago, and Herman opened a drugstore on Irving Park Boulevard. "He had terrible depressions," my father told me in his croaky voice. "There were days when he couldn't even get out of bed. He'd pull down the shades and draw the covers over his head, and that's how I'd find him when I came home from school. He had what he called the sad Russian gene. He always saw the dark side of the moon."

The Sad Russian gene: that explained a lot. It ran in the family. My father was an only child with two distracted parents who never managed to adapt to the New World—"a latchkey kid," as he describes himself, wandering the countryside of rural Indiana and catching toads in the muddy streams. At daybreak he rose and delivered newspapers on horseback. His mother was never around; she studied and studied for the pharmacy exam, failing so many times that the instructor finally passed her out of pity. ("Not again, Mrs. Atlas!") What she lacked in brains she made up for in looks. "I remember I found her once flirting with a student. She was vain about her age and pretended I was her little brother. I could tell she wanted to get rid of me. Finally she made me go home."

As dawn creeps through the windows of his hospital room, he's still muttering to himself, "'The falcon cannot hear the falconer.'" What does this poem mean to him? I wonder, huddled beneath my thin blanket. Somehow the line is key: he feels cut off from the world, unable to communicate with other people. He makes fun of his stilted epistolary style, inherited from his father—"'Yours of the 14th in hand, I hasten to reply . . .'"—but it reflects his distance from even those closest to him, his wife and his two sons. It's not that he's remote or forbidding; his emotions are easily tapped, and he cries with little provocation. At weddings, funerals, birthday parties, he's the first one to reach for his handkerchief. Listening to a concert in a church basement on a Sunday afternoon, he sits on a folding chair in his brown wool suit and dabs his eyes, overcome by the stately cadences of Handel's *Water Music*. He even weeps at my college commencement ceremony, when I stand up with a thousand other black-robed graduates to receive my diploma.

No, it's not a lack of emotion that stunts my father's response to the world; it's an excess of emotion. He feels too much. I think back to his sixtieth anniversary party, in a Doubletree Inn suite in Chicago four years earlier. We had flown in from New York, and my parents had flown in from California. The dinner was at a private room in the hotel. Mother was elegant as usual, in a white linen ensemble of trousers and a jacket with ivory buttons; father was in a khaki suit, a white shirt, and a paisley tie. It was a small party: two couples they'd known forever; a widow—one of many in their circle—and my father's secretary, a refined old lady who was close to eighty herself. All the rest of their friends were dead or down in Florida sitting on lawn chairs in the sun.

It was a touching scene. The grandchildren recited a list of "The Top Ten Things We Like Best about Grandma and Grandpa." ("The multitude of breakfast foods which Grandma always offers us to make sure there is exactly what we want"; "Grandpa's photographs, which, after all the struggling with the zoom lens, tend to wind up minus an arm or leg"). I read aloud from my parents' letters to me over the years, alternating between them: "I continue to knock myself out on the tennis court playing with other wizened gray-haired men in blue nylon track suits . . ."; "We had a very good dinner, featuring coq au vin from a recipe furnished by my hairdresser, Teddy . . ." My father's oldest friend, Jerry, sang a halting rendition of "Gonna Make a Sentimental Journey," changing the words to recall their joint honeymoon sixty years before. Then my father made a brief speech, recounting his good fortune in marrying into the Glassenberg clan. "We're more attached to each other than ever," my mother said, trying not to cry. "We're two lovebirds."

After dinner, we went across the street to Jerry's apartment to see his art collection. Through the wide picture windows, a glistening river of traffic flowed along Lake Shore Drive. It was a stunning collection—Gris, Braque, de Kooning, Chagall—but what stayed with me was the pair of Rolls-Royces we passed in the garage on the way back to our hotel—his and hers Silver Clouds, half-cloaked beneath canvas shrouds, that belonged to one of the great dynastic families of Chicago. Both the patriarch and the matriarch had recently died. I found the sight of these shiny, powerful monuments to vast wealth unsettling. They all go into the dark, but their cars stay in the garage.

The next day we made a pilgrimage to our old house in Evanston, on a quiet, tree-lined cul-de-sac by the beach. A new house had gone up on the lot that was once our yard—the only thing that had changed since they sold the house and moved to California. There was a FOR SALE sign next to the driveway. Maybe I could emulate Albert Brooks in that movie, *Mother*, about the fortyish guy who decides to move back in with his mother after his marriage falls apart. He sets up his room just like it was when he was a teenager, unpacks his pennants and trophies, puts the Four Tops on the CD player at ear-splitting volume. "I want to try to recapture a feeling," he says to his baffled old mom. It's a thought that's crossed my mind. I could buy our house, install the parents in the master bedroom, persuade my brother to join me in our old rooms. Kind of like Biff and Happy in *Death of a Salesman*.

My mother peered over the bamboo gate, trying to see into the walled patio. "Yoo-hoo," she called. The rest of us hesitated, not wishing to intrude, but she was determined. After a few minutes, a pretty blond woman in her fifties came to the gate. My mother explained who we were. The woman was glad to see us; she had always been curious about the original owners, she said. She quieted her madly barking dog and ushered us inside.

The children stood silently in my old bedroom, with its Formica desk and cabinets, its pennant-adorned walls, its closet stuffed with athletic gear—clearly a boy's room still. I could see by the look of bafflement on their faces the new fact they were struggling to absorb: their father had been a child, too.

We gathered in front of the house, and the lady who owned it now snapped our photograph. Then it was time to go our separate ways. We were heading for the airport to catch a flight back to New York. My parents were staying on for a few days. We stood beside our rented car. "Good-bye, Sonny," my father said, laying a hand on my neck. I remember how he looked away and draped a hand over his brow to hide the tears in his eyes.

Did he know that he had been a good father? That his sons felt loved? I doubt such an ordinary achievement registered with him. In his own mind, he was a "loser," convinced that his main legacy was having presided over the diminution of the family nest egg, the modest fortune my grandfather built up in a prosperous career as a wool merchant. Saddled with the responsibility of protecting the trust, my father timidly allowed the bankers who served as collateral trustees to let it dwindle away; it never occurred to him to challenge the will. So, okay: it's true that he didn't have a head for business. He has this refrain: *If only Grandpa Sam hadn't sold that parcel of land in Palm Springs . . . If only I hadn't sold Brunswick just before bowling got popular . . .* What makes it harder is that so many of his friends were big successes: the head of a cardiology unit, the founder of a textile company, a partner in one of the mammoth LaSalle Street law firms. My father was refused tenure at Northwestern Medical School; he never had the stomach for political infighting. By declaring himself out of the game early, he wouldn't have to play.

He had built up a solid practice, but he never seemed to have his heart in it. Wednesday afternoons were reserved for his weekly doubles game; he was always home by six and devoted weekends to his cerebral hobbies: his oboe, his bonsai trees, his books. What he'll leave—it occurs to me as I brush my teeth in the hospital bathroom, the green metal walls and silver toilet basin like a Pullman sleeping car—is the essence of his nature, the traits we've come to refer to in our family as "Donaldian." He was a crusader against all forms of intellectual laziness: he loathed television (except for *Omnibus* and, later on, *Masterpiece Theatre*); inveighed tirelessly against "platitudes" and "banalities" (*Reader's Digest*, the radio commentator Paul Harvey, the pious sermonizing of suburban rabbis); hated jokes but loved humor. Watching the *Jack Benny Show* (which somehow escaped his prohibition against TV), he used to laugh until tears came to his eyes.

If he was a failure in his own eyes, in the eyes of others he was a lively, even charismatic presence. His friends revered him for the very qualities he deprecated in himself: he was an oddball, an original. He had other pleasures in life besides getting and spending. He intoned *The Love Song of J. Alfred Prufrock* with relish, turning Eliot's bleak lines ("I grow old . . . I grow old . . . / I shall wear the bottoms of my trousers rolled") into comedy. Steve and I gained points with our friends for having such a father. They gravitated toward him, drawn by his playful irony. Whenever my friend Richard was over, my father would entertain him by reciting the dour aphorisms of Richard's dad: "You're kicking field goals at twilight." "You're rocking a dead baby."

He was also a gifted mimic. At the dinner table, he would entertain us with imitations of his patients, like the Parkinsonian whose arm trembled and spastically shot out from his side. But when he saw this patient shaving in front of a hospital mirror, my father marveled at the way he could, with a tremendous effort, bring the razor to his face and execute a swift, miraculously accurate swipe against his cheek before his arm flew off again, waving like a lobster's antenna. Then there was the one we called the Bird Man of the Palmolive Building, a tremulous elderly elevator operator afflicted with nervous tics whose darting head and blinking eyes my father had mastered through long study. When I got on the elevator one day and came face-to-face with the original, I was stunned by the exactitude of my father's performance. None of this, I contemplated, would survive him. His mannerisms, his pronouncements, his turns of phrase—his Donaldian essence—all were soon to vanish from the earth.

"Tuck your shirt in," he says, looking me up and down as if I'm thirteen and on my way to a bar mitzvah. "The doctor is coming."

I sat working on my laptop in the solarium, watching schoolchildren play soccer on a field across the street. It was the beginning of summer, and the grass was emerald green; the redbrick buildings of Boston, elegant against the robin's-egg blue sky tufted with white clouds. Planes, silent through the plate-glass windows, floated toward Logan Airport. Death was in the vicinity—one afternoon as I sat answering my e-mail an elderly man in hospital pajamas tottered in with his nurse, pushing a walker before him, and released a thin stream of diarrhea on the carpet of the solarium. "Don't worry about it, Mr. Stedman," the nurse said cheerfully. "We'll deal with that." I didn't mind. I saw it as all part of life now. The old man defecated; the children kicked the black-and-white soccer ball. The air was so clear that I could make out the ball's octagonal pattern from seven floors above the field. I held my breath and kept on typing.

I quickly became accustomed to the hospital, to the rhythms of my days. I sat in my father's room, talking to him and, when he slept, to my stoical mother. I grew to enjoy the basement cafeteria: the crummy food, the cheeseburgers in aluminum wrap, the hardened onion rings in their cardboard containers beneath the infrared heating lights; the stillness and emptiness of the big room with its long tables and metal chairs when I went down for a late dinner after the nurses had put my father to bed for the night. It was a world away from the pressures of New York—like being in a belowground atomic bunker. The only newspaper I read was *USA Today*, obtainable from a vending machine. Otherwise I was cut off from the glut of data that normally crowded into my consciousness each day demanding attention—e-mail and magazines and Internet babble. Cell phones were prohibited on the ward because they interfered with all the electronic gadgetry keeping end-of-the-line patients alive for a few more weeks or months or days. It was weirdly satisfying to have my life so regimented, so basic, so stripped down to the essentials.

It took nearly a week to get a definitive diagnosis: it wasn't a brain tumor after all but a brain abscess. Instead of being sent down to the operating room, my father was put on a heavy regimen of antibiotics and shipped off to a rehabilitation hospital west of Boston. It was there that he spent the summer.

The New England Rehabilitation Center was in Woburn, off Route 128, behind a mall with a Radio Shack, a Boston Chicken, a Rite Aid. (*Woeburn*, I always thought to myself when I drove there.) It was a cheerless brick building, and the patients weren't all old: there were bikers who'd totaled their motorcycles and broken many bones; survivors of grisly car accidents; emphysematous Vietnam vets. The latter were dedicated smokers and clustered on the patio out back beside the parking lot, sitting around picnic tables and filling plastic ashtrays with their butts. Even outdoors, the stale odor of cigarette smoke hung in the warm summer air. When the weather was fine, my brother and I would take turns wheeling my father out to the patio, where he sat turning his face to the sun in the New England June.

At first he seemed to be improving. He still couldn't move his left arm, which was now in a sling, but he could make his way slowly around the exercise room, clutching his walker and urged on by the physical therapist, a plump kindly woman who treated every step as if it were a momentous achievement. "Excellent, Dr. Atlas!" she would cry.

"Keep going. I want to see you make it all the way to the door." Despite his baggy sweatpants, foam-padded slippers, and wrinkled L. L. Bean shirt, he was still Dr. Atlas, still a semblance of the purposeful, vigorous man he'd once been. "I think he's making progress, don't you?" my mother would say hopefully as Étienne, the muscular Haitian nurse, wrestled him back onto his bed.

He was better off than his roommate, Mr. Walters, who had been disabled by a stroke and could hardly speak. A handsome man with a head of silken white hair, he was frustrated by his inability to communicate and rolled agitatedly around on his bed, muttering to himself, flailing his arms as if he were groping down a dark passage. The intensity of his need unnerved me. "Can I help you, Mr. Walters?" I asked him. "Is there something I can get you?" He opened his mouth and groaned: "Uh-h-h-h-h . . ." But no words came. He stared at me with wide anguished eyes, trying to will his guttural utterances into comprehensible speech by the sheer force of his gaze. It was a relief when a nurse came and pulled the curtain between the two beds, shielding us from his mute, accusing stare. *What happened?* I imagined him demanding. *Who did this? You want to get me something? How about my life back?*

My father himself spoke less and less. He found it an effort to make conversation, and answered our solicitous questions about his progress with a perfunctory "I'm all right" or "I feel okay." Whenever I asked if he was comfortable, he would nod his head yes. One day I recounted to him an exchange I'd had with thirteen-year-old William. "Why don't you talk to me more?" I'd asked him, worried by his laconic manner. "I have nothing to say," he replied. My father adored this story. Sitting in his wheelchair on the patio, he would suddenly announce, "I have nothing to say." There was something about the simplicity of Will's statement—perhaps its defiant pride, its refusal to play the social game—that delighted him. He could make his own infirmity a principle.

Sometimes, though, he would come to life, some buried ancient memory activated by a neuronal surge in his brain. "Can you remember the mnemonic for the bones of the wrist?" my brother asked him one day, probing his medical-school synapses. My father, stretched out on his hospital bed, eyes closed, recited in a strong voice: "Never pull down Tillie's pants, her momma might come home." He still enjoyed a good line. "Why doesn't he open his eyes?" my mother said as she spoon-fed my father. "He's afraid you'll try to stuff apple sauce in there," my brother said. My father smiled: "You're a funny fellow, Steve." Another time, sitting motionless on the patio, he stirred to life when the subject of my humiliating efforts to learn a musical instrument came up. In high school, I had taken lessons and successively abandoned the piano, the flute, and the mandolin. "That's right," my father, himself an accomplished musician, said happily. "One of your music teachers told me you were completely tone-deaf." To entertain him, I dredged up another instance of failure: "And then I tried to paint, remember, Dad? I did that abstract drip painting with the white square in the middle that Grandma Liz thought was so profound and hung on her living room wall." "Awful, awful," he intoned with a shake of his head. Was he enjoying this exercise in belittlement too much?

I was startled—and a little embarrassed—by my stubborn hunger for my father's approval. He was eighty-seven, after all; I was fifty-two, a father myself. Wasn't I a little old to be dependent on his good opinion, still fishing for praise and trying to impress him with my accomplishments? Most men my age no longer even had fathers; many didn't have any parents at all. "My mom would have been delirious," a parentless writer confided to me after his book hit the best-seller list. "I try to believe they know about it," he added wistfully. Having no parents sharply diminishes one's circle of uncritical admirers. "They're your number one fans," my friend said dolefully. "Now I'm an orphan." And if they weren't, if the relationship wasn't so good, you had to deal with what psychologists like to call "unfinished business"—who wants to feel angry toward someone who's dead? My father couldn't stand his mother—a "cannibalistic old woman," in his own harsh words, who once lay down in front of her door in an effort to prevent him from leaving after one of his dutiful Sunday visits. But I'll never forget his face as he stumbled away from her fresh grave: bewildered, stunned, *afraid.*

Even before he got sick, I remember coming home from work one day and finding my father, on a visit from the West Coast, dozing on the sofa. I was seized with a premonitory sensation of emptiness, a prefig-urement of loss, a pang of abandonment primal in its intensity; I had last felt this way, it occurred to me, when my parents left me alone at Camp Shewahmegon forty years ago and drove off down the dusty road in their white Lincoln, leaving me by the door of my bunk with a knapsack and a sleeping bag. How would I ever get through the night without them?

When the father of a close friend died in his late eighties I spent a week sitting shivah—the Jewish tradition of prolonged mourning that requires the bereaved to gather in the presence of family and a rabbi each night at sundown to read through the Kaddish, the ancient Hebrew prayer for the dead. As we stood in the parlor of his Greenwich Village town house, surrounded by Impressionist paintings and leather-bound books, I saw my friend as the boy he'd been, vulnerable in his yarmulke, growing up above a corner grocery store in the Bronx. When we got to the part where the prayer book says, "A final separation awaits every relationship, no matter how tender. Someday we shall have to drop every object to which our hands now cling," I nearly wept myself.

At night, sitting beside my father's bed in the hospital, I would think of my grandparents' house on Laurel Avenue in Wilmette, Illinois, where the cracked sidewalk petered out by the golf course and my fin-gers turned crimson from the raspberries I picked off a gnarled bush in the yard. That was forty years ago. Yet I still ache for them.

My parents weren't nostalgic. They were suffocated by their immigrant parents, who lived a few blocks away on either side of them in Chicago. Every Sunday we had the obligatory Sunday dinner at the home of one or the other. The boiled chicken, the borscht and gefilte fish, the fiestaware on the kitchen table, the family portraits in silver frames, the nut bowls on the coffee table, the plastic-covered couch: how oppressive it must have been for my parents, a prison of Jewish provincialism. I *liked* these occasions, liked watching the *Ed Sullivan Show* on the Magnavox. But I didn't have to listen to grandma complain to her mama's-boy son: "You never got heartburn when you lived at home."

Until a few years ago, my parents visited us twice a year, flying into New York—I would pick them up at the airport. When there was a health crisis Steve and I racked up frequent-flier miles shuttling back and forth across the country, consulting long-distance from their kitchen with doctors in New York or Boston. When maintaining the California house became untenable, they moved to what was essentially an old people's dorm in a town they'd never even laid eyes on before they arrived at Brookhaven with all the furniture that could fit in three rooms.

Their journey reflects a generational trend: quarantined in geriatric ghettos, stacked up in Florida condominiums, or corralled into "gated communities" in the California desert, they're essentially on their own. Why can't we be like the Italians, who live in the same house for generations and always seem to have a resident *nonna* in the kitchen? When I was a child, the grandparents were a fixture on the scene: my grandmother's house was full of odd relatives, cousins and nieces and nephews of such complex lineage that I could hardly follow my mother's patient explications of who they were: "Sylvia is the daughter of Grandma Liz's second cousin once removed who was married to Leon the dentist from Valparaiso." I was fond of these maiden aunts and eccentric uncles, like my grandmother's brother, Benny, who lived in the basement and made beautiful ornate clocks out of copper and old parts. They're gone now. Only my mother's cousins Florence and Emma survive, dispersed to assisted-living facilities in Oakland and somewhere in Oregon—wherever their children happened to settle. Gone with them is a way of life—the extended multigenerational network of family and friends that stayed within driving range of one another and functioned as communities. On holidays they traveled from neighboring towns or states, the backseats of their cars laden with food—turkey, fruit salad, and pies covered in tinfoil. In the living room, Florence's husband, Harry, who owned a camera store, set up the projector, loaded the slides into the circular holder, and showed us the vacation photos of their cross-country trip to the Grand Canyon. We sat down to raucous dinners, everyone talking at once. When we hugged good-bye on the front stoop—I can still remember the fragrant warmth of Emma's fur coat pressed against my cheek—we lingered in the cold, our breath visible in the porch light. Finally it was time to go. I slid into the chilly vinyl-covered backseat and fell asleep. Then we got in our cars and drove away.

My parents have each other. But what happens when one of them ends up alone? "If one of us goes first—" my mother says one Sunday night over the phone, trying to prepare me. "What other scenario is there?" I interrupt. We both laugh nervously.

My father's oldest friend, Jerry, had been calling up almost daily all summer from Chicago, asking after my father's condition and insisting he wanted to fly out for a visit. They had known each other since high school. Jerry's father was a peddler on the West Side who sold paper bags, wrapping paper, and twine to merchants. Jerry went off to Northwestern with my father, in the midst of the Depression, but his family pressured him to drop out; his father and brothers had decided to form their own paper and cardboard business, and they needed Jerry to give a hand. "I thought he was crazy," my father had told me once. "Businesses were closing, banks were failing. I felt the country was on the verge of socialism or even communism and that private enterprise was doomed." The only safe thing, my father argued, was education. So he went off to medical school while Jerry joined the family business. Now Jerry's name is on a Michigan Avenue building; his company is listed on the New York Stock Exchange. He built a museum in the city. Mayor Daley named a street after him. "Why didn't you invest in Jerry's business?" I asked my father. He shook his head. "I don't know. Jerry was my friend . . ."

Jerry flew into Boston one boiling day in July and took a taxi out to Woburn to see my father (negotiating the tariff down from forty dollars to thirty-five). My brother brought a video camera and taped their reunion.

JERRY: He used to get all the girls.

DONALD: No, he would get the girls, and I remember one specific girl: Ruth Schwartz. I was dating her and all of a sudden he's necking with her in the backseat.

STEVE (to Jerry): So you just stole your best friend's girl?

DONALD: That's him.

JERRY: It worked both ways. We both liked a girl who lived on the West Side. Edith Borowitz.

DONALD (coughing, amid much laughter): She wore a corset.

JERRY: She was a beautiful girl. She'd say, "Well, I'm busy. I'm going out with Donald."

It wasn't a long visit, maybe an hour. Jerry was in robust health, but he was eighty-seven, too. Their leave-taking was painful to watch: like my father, Jerry thought of himself as unsentimental, a tough-hearted old bird from Chicago. But they both sensed—no, knew—they wouldn't see each other again. They embraced, and turned away. Jerry hurried out of the room. My father sat in his wheelchair, staring off into space. His face looked ruined, devastated. He didn't know my brother had left the camera on. "He came to see you," my mother said softly.

She was by his side every day, driving over from Brookhaven in the old Volvo they'd shipped across the country from California. For lunch she brought him a lobster roll from McDonald's: "He doesn't like this hospital food." But the strain was beginning to show. When I helped her up the walk to her door at night I was alarmed to discover that I could wrap my hand around her bony arm. Her days behind the wheel were nearly over; one morning when she failed to show up at the rehab center my brother drove around frantically looking for her and finally spotted the car in downtown Lexington. My mother had gotten dizzy on the way over and called a cab to take her home.

We begged her to stay home for a day now and then, just to get some rest, but she wouldn't listen. "He needs me," she said. "He doesn't eat if I'm not here." One day she showed up in a blue silk skirt with a matching scarf and shoes, gold hoop earrings, a string of pearls around her neck. Her lipstick had been carefully applied. "What's the deal?" I said. "Why are you so dressed up?"

"It's our anniversary," she said shyly.

They had been married for sixty-four years, and had known each other for even longer. In the family archives was a home movie of my mother's Sweet Sixteen party at her parents' house in Wilmette. The footage was grainy and jerky—like watching an old Chaplin film—but there, heading downstairs to the basement, was my father, nineteen, with another girl (Edith Borowitz?) on his arm.

"We both dated other people," my mother told me one night when we were sitting at the table in her cramped kitchen, "but I always knew he was the one." They had been through difficult patches, but one of the things about being married for sixty-four years was that you could be out of phase at one point and then develop a new emotional alignment as you grew older. During their last three decades—a far longer interval than most marriages lasted—my mother and father were deeply in love. "And you remained, uh, faithful to each other all those years?" I asked. "As far as I know," my mother answered cautiously. "Certainly *I* was." They were rarely out of each other's sight. I remember her telling me, with a trace of pride, about the widows from my father's Great Books class who were always calling up and asking "Is Don home?" She had a husband and they didn't.

At Brookhaven, the women outnumber the men by something like four or five to one. They sit in the dining room in groups of four, joined by the rare elderly gentleman in a sport jacket and tie who has somehow defied the demographics. It's so hard to remember that these people were once young—that they not only had lives, but sex lives. One day I passed an octogenarian couple talking in the parlor. Their chairs were close together, their knees almost touching. The man's knotty hands rested on his cane. The woman's white haired head was bent coquettishly as she leaned forward to listen. "They both lost their spouses recently," my mother said when I described them. "They're hot and heavy."

Apart from the lopsided gender differential and the plain meals— "Baked Scrod with Lite Crumb Topping," "Wiener Schnitzel with Lemon Garnish"—Brookhaven is an elder-paradise. The public rooms are light and sunny, with sturdy furniture in Laura Ashley plush; there's a woodworking shop, a crafts room, an art studio, a well-stocked gift shop, a library with periodicals and shelves of books-on-tape. "The Harvard of assisted-living facilities," my father calls it. Residential wings are named after New England prep schools and Ivy League colleges: Amherst, Exeter, Dartmouth. The wide carpeted hallways are adorned with prints of Boston Harbor and Concord by John Singleton and Fitz Hugh Lane.

The place hums. "Every effort has been made to keep the 'natives' active and content," writes Isabel Abbott in *The Voice,* a monthly featuring poems, stories, puzzles, a column on "Brookhaven Newsmakers," and a page of book reviews. "The myriad of activities is designed to appeal to every taste: films, lectures, music programs, exercise programs, seminars on a wide range of topics." The Calendar of Events is crowded: on any given day, you can sign up for Living with Arthritis, Knit & Stitch, or Stretchercise; go on a field trip ("Let's Do Lunch at Kelby's in Saugus," "There is still room on the bus for the upcoming trip to the swan boats"). After dinner, residents drift into the spacious parlor for "Sing Along with Margie Miller." Holding songbooks open on their laps, they raise their quavery voices in ragged unison as Margie leads them through the old standards: "Way Down upon the Swanee River," "Row, Row, Row Your Boat," "Home Sweet Home." It's a geriatric summer camp. "We like it here," my mother explains. "When you're surrounded by other old people, you don't think of yourself as old."

The only ominous signs are the motorized wheelchairs parked out front and the "In Memory" column of *The Voice.* And this disquieting ritual: on days when a Brookhaven resident has died, the name of the deceased is written on a card and placed on a table by the entrance to the dining room, beside a vase that holds a single rose.

He was receding before our eyes. His life had narrowed down to a few pleasures: the lobster roll from McDonald's; the Sony Walkman we bought him, along with a few Mozart and Bach CDs; the visits from his grandchildren. He could no longer read, or even listen to my mother read; he couldn't focus on his favorite TV program, the *NewsHour with Jim Lehrer.* He slept more and more each day. The world was growing dim.

In the middle of August, my brother called me in Vermont. "Dad's back in the hospital." He sounded weary. I had driven back and forth to Boston a few times over the summer in my parents' other car, a mottled green 1979 Peugeot that rasped over the Green Mountains, emitting plumes of black smoke on the steep inclines. But my brother had been the one holding down the fort. He was the one at most of the meetings with the doctors, the social workers, the staff psychiatrist, the case worker; the one who had driven my mother to the hospital on days when she didn't feel up to driving over herself. "What now?" I said.

They had diagnosed a heart fibrillation and taken him back to Beth Israel in an ambulance; my mother rode alongside.

I got in the Peugeot and drove to Boston on Route 2, past the Indian souvenir shops and the paper factories and the sleepy towns with desolate motels on the outskirts, until the road widened and became a highway and Boston loomed up in the distance, the city on the hill. When I walked into my father's room, he opened his eyes in surprise and said, "What are you doing here?" He talked as if he had cotton in his mouth: "Wha-ar ou oo-ing here?"

"I came to see you," I said brightly. "How are you?"

I had to lean down to hear his answer. Finally I figured it out: "A little paralysis goes a long way." He laughed, a silent, mirthful laugh, baring his teeth in a grimace. His sparse hair was pasted to his head. His arm was bloated, purple.

Over the next few days, Steve and I sat in on meetings with an army of end-game specialists—grievance counselors and hospice workers and geriatric physicians whose business was, as one fresh-faced young chief resident explained, "the opposite of an obstetrician: they bring people into the world. We ease them out of it." (Who would want to go into such a peculiar subspecialty?) Somber-faced, soft-voiced, they were practiced in the ways of death. After many hushed conferences in the solarium, we agreed that my father should be put on a heavy dose of antibiotics to try and knock out the pneumonia. But we didn't want "extraordinary measures" to be taken in the event of heart failure; we didn't want him revived.

As this last act was unfolding, I picked up the phone one day and learned that a good friend had just dropped dead of a heart attack while climbing Mount Rainier. He was fifty-one years old. A few days later, having returned to Vermont—it was August, and I was trying to have a vacation—I got in the car with Anna, drove to Albany, boarded the 6 A.M. train to New York, jumped in a cab to our apartment, changed into dark clothes, and rode the subway down to Trinity Church on Wall Street for the funeral, attended the reception in Brooklyn Heights, and hurried back to Penn Station to catch the train back to Albany and retrieve the car from the parking lot and drive home to Vermont on the dark back roads, arriving there at midnight. It hardly sank in that he was dead. Laurie: he had been terrific on skis, a sophisticated journalist who knew his way around the European capitals and had four phone numbers on his card—home, office, London office, mobile. But he'd been going through a tough divorce and was smoking again. As I stood on my porch that night, looking up at the stars, the fireflies on the lawn like a reflection of the sky, I could almost sense the world closing in over my head; crickets chirred in the inky dark, reminding me of childhood summers in Illinois when I rode my bike through the leafy streets after dinner and waited for my life to begin. Now it was, however gradually, coming to an end.

Later that week, we were in New Haven for a wedding. (So far I'd driven three thousand miles that month, and there was still a week to go.) It was the second marriage for bride and groom—one was a widower, one was divorced. Between them they had numerous children. When the minister recited Ecclesiastes—"There is a time to be born, a time to die, a time for every purpose under heaven"—an old friend sitting next to me in the pew leaned over and whispered: "This is the second time I've heard those words today." In the morning he had attended the funeral of a neighbor's father.

The deathwatch in Boston, meanwhile, wouldn't let up. I was on my way to the general store one afternoon for milk when my cell phone rang. "He's going down," my brother said. I pulled over to the side of the road, feeling my heart speed up. The massive dose of antibiotic wasn't working; they had taken another CAT scan of my father's lungs and found they'd gotten worse, not better; he was drowning in his own fluids. "There's nothing more they can do. He's not gonna get to his next birthday"—his eighty-eighth, a week away.

I drove home and told Anna. We talked about my father's long life, about my mother, about the gardener and the bushes that needed mulching . . . Life was going on. An hour later, I got back in the Peugeot and started up the dirt road toward the general store; I had never gotten the milk. Two hundred yards from the house, the car stopped. The gas pedal felt loose. I gunned it a few times. Nothing. I walked home and called the local mechanic from Redeemed Repair, the automobile-repair shop in town that was run by born-again Christians. It was only as I trudged up the road to meet the tow-truck guy and saw the broken-down Peugeot by the side of the road that I began to weep.

A few minutes later, the mechanic pulled up in a flatbed truck. He wore a Blue Seal Feed cap and had an unfiltered cigarette in his mouth. Over the pocket of his blue denim shirt was stitched the name *Clyde*. He opened the hood and pawed around, probing the tangle of wires and tubes with a sure hand that reminded me of Dr. Wu, the chief surgeon, examining my father. "Your transmission's shot," Clyde said after a while. "This thing ain't going nowhere for a while—maybe ever."

I went around to the back of the car and opened the trunk. Inside was a black nylon garment bag that I'd brought back from New York. It contained Will's gray Brooks Brothers suit; my daughter Molly's black dress; Anna's black dress; my charcoal suit. Clyde backed up, lowered the ramp of his truck, and fastened a big iron hook to the bottom of the car. Then he winched it up and drove off in a cloud of dust.

The next morning I drove to Boston in a rental van. My head was empty. I listened to the radio, the oldies station from Pittsfield, and when Otis Redding's "Sittin' on the Dock of the Bay" came on, I was ecstatic. Only for the briefest instant did I feel guilty about being happy driving to my father's deathbed. It was a mindless, animal happiness— the happiness of the horse galloping in the meadow, the bird singing in the tree. I was alive.

My father was asleep—or unconscious—when I walked into his room. When he woke up and saw me, he frowned. It had to be obvious to him that my sudden arrival wasn't a good sign. But it could also have been that he didn't want to put me to any trouble. "Go about your business," he mumbled. For him, one of the most important aspects of parenting was to make the child feel no obligation whatever to the parents. His parents had oppressed and crowded him; he would set his children free—whether we wanted to be free or not. It comforted me to sit by his bedside. I read the *Boston Globe,* my mother knitted; my father—I thought—had fallen asleep, or whatever it was that he did now. Suddenly I heard him say, in a clear, emphatic voice: "Bellow."

I looked up. "What was that?" I had published a biography of Saul Bellow a few months before, and had been complaining to him the night I slept over in the hospital about some tough reviews I'd gotten. "Bellow," he repeated now. "Good."

We had agreed to remove my father from life support when the time came, and arranged for him to be admitted to what was delicately referred to as the "nursing facility"—the basement of Brookhaven where patients who'd had strokes or were in other ways disabled were kept. My brother had gone away for a couple of days to visit friends up on Lake Champlain; he needed a rest. I conferred once more with the attending physician, a strikingly attractive woman with short-cropped hair. "Cute lady," my father commented. An hour later, a nurse came in and pulled a tube out of his arm. She wrapped it around the IV pole like a sailor flinging a rope onto a ship's deck and trundled off, pushing the pole in front of her. For the first time in two months, my father was on his own, unattached, unmoored.

He wanted to go back to Brookhaven: "Home," he called it, even though he'd only lived there for seven months.

While we waited for the ambulance, I read him the Yeats poem he'd been memorizing, "The Second Coming," then others I knew he liked: "Crazy Jane," "The Wild Swans at Coole," "Sailing to Byzantium." I was about to skip the lines about old age—"That is no country for old men", "An aged man is but a paltry thing, a tattered coat upon a stick, unless / Soul clap its hands and sing." And then I thought, *Why? He understands. There's no shame in old age; this is where he found his courage.* When I got to the end of the poem, he called out, with startling ardor, "Marvelous! Marvelous!"

Around mid-afternoon, a two-woman ambulance team came up in their blue uniforms. Burly, muscular, but gentle, they lifted him off the bed, careful of his sticklike limbs, and stretched him out on a gurney, then wheeled him to the elevator; my mother gathered up her knitting and followed behind. I said good-bye and dragged a garbage bag crammed with my father's belongings down to the car in the hospital garage. Slippers, shirts, pajamas, bandages, his arm sling, the plastic boots he wore to improve his circulation, vials of drugs. I would meet them at Brookhaven.

I had driven a few blocks when it hit me. I pulled over to the curb, laid my head on the wheel, and wept. I cried as I'd never cried before, deep wrenching sobs that made it hard for me to breathe.

When I got to Brookhaven, he was already installed in his room. The sour smell of decay hung in the air. I loitered around for a while, sitting in the chair by his bedside and listening to him breathe. I couldn't figure out whether to stay or not, but the nurse told me you could never be sure. "It could be days."

Finally, around ten, I decided to go. I'd be staying at my brother's house, just five minutes away, in case anything happened. I read Dad *The Love Song of J. Alfred Prufrock* one last time, but I couldn't tell if he heard it or not. Then I kissed him on his forehead and walked out into the summer night.

I was lying in bed the next morning around eight, listening to birds chirp in the yard, when the phone rang. I knew right away what it was. My sister-in-law, Robin, answered and then called my name. It was the nurse from the night before. "I'm sorry to have to tell you that your father passed away a few minutes ago."

My heart was pounding as I got dressed and drove over to Brookhaven. I hurried up to my mother's apartment and knocked on the door. She answered it in her nightgown. "Mom," I said, embracing her body. It felt so brittle! "I'm sorry, Mom."

"No, dear, no," she cried piteously. "I'm not ready yet. I'm not ready. I told him not to go." We sat down on the couch and held each other while my mother wept. I was dry-eyed, eager to get away from this scene of grief and back down to my father. I wanted to see him again.

When I got to his room, he was lying on his bed. His head looked very small, and his teeth protruded more than in life. He reminded me of photographs of the Bog Man. It wasn't him anymore, but it was. I bent down and put my face up against his cheek; a kindly orderly at Beth Israel had given him a shave that afternoon, and his skin was nice and smooth. I touched my lips to his forehead: it was cool. Cold. The nurse stood in the doorway. He had been awake and asked for breakfast, she said, but "all of a sudden he got pale and stopped breathing. It just happened like that."

She gave me the name of a local funeral home. I was uncomfortable making the call while the row of patients (residents? inmates?) sat in their wheelchairs silently observing me—drooling, their heads lolling to the side, their arms crossed in their laps. I couldn't make this call in front of them: I told the nurse about my qualms, and she led me to a phone in her office.

When I was done making the arrangements, I went back to his room. He lay there —no longer "he" but a corpse now. The departure of my father's life from his body was at once a great mystery and the most ordinary thing in the world. I had never been in the presence of a dead body before. I marveled at the radical fact of absence, the finality of it all. Not a word, no directive, no sign would ever issue from him again.

I lounged in a chair, my leg over the arm, at ease. Then my sister-in-law came in with my mother. She stood over him and tried to take it in. "I'm not ready to let you go, bunny," she said, talking to him in the same intimate, bantering voice I'd been hearing all summer. "We had a good time, didn't we, darly? We laughed and laughed and had a good time. But I didn't want you to go yet. I didn't want you to go." She kissed his head and turned to me, a confused look on her face. "How did I let him get away?" she said. She went over to the window and looked out at the green lawn, the green shrubs visible at eye level through the basement window. "Dear, I know this sounds strange," she said in a half-whisper, "but I feel like he's still breathing."

On the bureau was a can of Gillette shaving cream that I'd bought the day before at Walgreen's. I was planning to give him a shave, but it was too late for that now. I would take it home and use it myself.

That afternoon I drove over to Worthen Funeral Home in Lexington and signed a lot of documents. The undertaker, a solemn young man with a fullback's build and a black suit, explained the "burial options" in a low murmurous voice—the voice of practiced unction. He led me into a showroom filled with mahogany caskets, cherrywood caskets, chrome-lined caskets with stuffed plush silk. Not for us: my father had chosen to be cremated. In another room was a selection of urns on a shelf. I chose a porcelain urn "in the midrange"—$375. "Very tasteful," the undertaker assured me. I had brought a suit for my father: even if you were going to be cremated, they made you put on a suit and shoes and tie. I guess it was for the guys who manned the crematorium, to make their job easier.

The funeral was held in the parlor at Brookhaven. A wind quintet we'd hired from the Longy School of Music played Mozart and Vivaldi as the guests filed in and took their seats in rows of folding chairs. There were Brookhaven residents, Anna's mother, my brother's tennis partners from his Sunday doubles game, a couple of old friends of ours from Boston, and Jerry, who had flown in from Chicago. He'd been invited to speak, and he told a story about my father. When they were in high school together, Jerry had to work such long hours at the family business that he never had time for any extracurricular activities. My father was an editor of the Carl Schurz High yearbook, and when he saw a blank next to Jerry's photograph where you were supposed to list the clubs and organizations you belonged to, he took pity on his friend. When Jerry got his copy of the yearbook and turned to his photograph, he was surprised to discover that he was a member of the marching band, the math club, and the debate team. My father had given him a life.

Every child has different parents, it's said, even if they're the same—time and circumstances alter the family dynamic. My brother was endowed with a happy disposition. I was endowed with a gloomy disposition. No one made us the way we are; we just turned out this way. It's nature, not nurture. Steve and I both spoke about my father, and we might as well have been speaking about different people. Steve focused on the California years. Recruited by a local activist who was struggling to found a clinic that would serve the Chicano community in downtown San Diego, my father had attended a meeting with the governor of the state, Pete Wilson, and persuaded him to hand over a government building for their use. Out of that meeting came the Chicano Free Clinic, with my father as its founding director. New clinics had been founded; my father had, in effect, started a movement. A plaque was going to be put up in his honor in the main center, now a busy hub that administered health care to twenty-five thousand people. He had never talked to me about the clinic.

I focused on why my father often found life so hard—a manifestation of the Sad Russian gene. He had a Spenglerian view of history (derived from actually having read Spengler) and believed the decline of the West was imminent; he had little faith in human nature, and liked to quote his uncle Albert, who would stand in a corner at family gatherings and, shaking his head, mutter "people, people, people." My father was happiest when he was alone, playing the English horn he'd bought from a secondhand dealer in London.

Everyone was in tears, even the musicians, as we filed out of the room to the mournful accompaniment of Bach's Concerto in E Minor.

The next day we got in our rented van with my mother and headed back to Vermont for the Labor Day weekend.

One afternoon I was on my way to Shaftsbury when I passed a pond by the side of the road where my father used to like to go when my parents came east for their annual summer visit. You could put a nickel in a dispensing machine and get a handful of pellets of fish food and feed it to the fat carp that swam lazily in circles. It reminded him of his solitary wanderings in Valparaiso as a child, when he would bicycle out to the countryside and fish. I sat by myself on a bench and watched the carp rise to swallow the pellets that I tossed in the water one by one. This would have been the week he was here. When Will was little, the two of them would spend hours by the pond together, feeding the fish. Will was too old for that pastime now; he was off playing golf with a friend. And Dad was gone. Only the carp remained, floating in the mineral-dark water. I sat there for a long time.

Two weeks later, the World Trade Center blew up.

Time

Exploring a cupboard, I find a fat manila envelope: "Personal Papers."
It's labeled in what I recognize as my late father's handwriting. I open it
up and pull out a jumbled wad of old papers—and I mean *old*. There
are crumbling yellow letters, photocopies, documents in Cyrillic,
envelopes with brittle cellophane windows, photographs curled at the
edges.

I study a photograph of my grandpa Herman, wearing a Trotsky-
like lorgnette, a high collar, a woolen suit and vest, his twenty-year-old
face surrounded by a sepia halo. It's affixed to a diploma with string and
a crumbling red seal. Handwritten in fine filigreed strokes are words in
Russian. Typed on a brittle, torn piece of paper is a translation:

*The bearer of this former student of Wawelberg's & Rotwand's High
Technical Schools in the city of Warsaw*

HIRSH ATLASBERG (H. Atlas)

*after graduating, the complete course of study in the above mentioned
school has been examined by a special appointed board . . .*

Here the page is torn. Below the tear it resumes:

The Faculty of the technical courses of the Moscow Industrial School in
memory of 25 years reigning of Emperor Alexander II meeting the 5th day
of October 1906, decided to bestow upon Atlasberg (Atlas) the degree of
TECHNIC OF MECHANICAL SPECIALTY with all the rights and
privileges attached to this degree.

Atlasberg's grades were in three categories: Excellent (polytechnical economy), Good (machine construction), and Satisfactory (chemical industry, commercial geography).

So we were once Atlasberg. Though why was the name "Atlas" there in parentheses? (Was the truncation already in the works, even before the routine lopping off of syllables at Ellis Island?) And Grandpa: I knew from my father that he had gotten a degree, despite strict prohibitions against Jews living in cities, much less attending school. But there was something uncanny about holding the actual document in my hand, with all its details to make the folkloric story real. (Wawelberg and Rotwand: what marvelous names. Did they have descendants living in Brooklyn? I was tempted to call information and ask if there was a listing for Rotwand.) My heart quickened as I pawed through the trove. I doubt these documents would have lasted another generation. Not that the children were negligent, but things get lost in every move; I couldn't keep track of my own papers. Had it not been for my chance discovery, this particular piece of family history would have disappeared forever.

I have a drawer full of pocket calendars, and when I leaf through them I rediscover lunches and dinners and even trips I'd forgotten all about. My desk is crammed with letters from people I haven't thought of in years, people who have dropped out of my life or moved away. But the treasure I've stumbled upon in its worn envelope goes much further

back; it contains the fossils of my family's history, like some fragile artifact unearthed by an archaeologist digging in the desert. Our story has
been given new life.

I open a spiral notebook, its cover faded to a pale brown: Whose
shaky scrawl is this? It must belong to my grandma Raya, Herman's
wife. She had a mania for self-improvement and enrolled year after year
in courses at DePaul College in the Loop. Her English was not good, but
she was fascinated by the language and was always trying to improve
her vocabulary. Pages and pages are filled with word definitions (*deprivation:* fact of being deprived) and usage exercises:

Diaphanous folds
Imperceptible fall
Immolate/Immolating/Immolated

It sounds like a poem, a haiku.

And there is poetry—real poetry—in the journal. On one page,
Grandma quotes from both Milton's *Comus* ("O welcome, pure-eyed
Faith, white-handed Hope") and Joyce Kilmer ("Poems are made by fools
like me, / But only God can make a tree"). There are also quotes from "Bow
Mar Shay" and Schopenhauer, in her own effortful transcription: "Every
man knows, and every woman too, that the year bring a rich assortment of
pain and sorrow to every soul; and that life is still a precious thing only
because the joys it gives are deep enough to be worth all the price we pay."

Another page lists courses: Psychology of Learning; Heredity and
Human Development; Introduction to Existentialism. She seems to
have enrolled in this last course; beneath it is the title of a textbook—*An
Introduction to Exist,* by Robert G. Olson—and an assignment: "Read 40
pages to agree and not agree."

Scattered amid Grandma's vocabulary building and syllabus jot-

tings are phone numbers of the long-dead: Ida Golden BR 4–9398 Ida
Klaitman KY 9–0354. *Ida:* women aren't named that anymore. The
names, and the phone numbers with lettered prefixes, reach out to me
across an abyss of time. There is also a number I recognize:

Donald Atlas 714-453-6444 To which she has mystifyingly added:
My Son.

I'm fascinated by the addresses in Grandma's book: 1734 N. Mozart,
3450 Marquette, 3200 Pratt. It occurs to me to drive around next time I'm
in Chicago and go visit them, parking my rented car out front. But why? I
know how they'll look: three-story flats in burgundy- and clay-colored
brick with sunporches jutting out in front. It's the idea that each of these
places was home, and that where my family once lived other families live
now—the homes are more permanent than their inhabitants.

Interspersed with this ancient data are personal notes:

Donald
May 9–1971
Talk today and he is conversing that he talk to Friday and I
remember that he did not talk to me on Sunday May the 9

I know I am a very sensitive person and impulsive but eager to please

I am searching deep in my heart where did I fail with my son and
his family is that because my love and devotion is very great for
them. I question myself all the time and always, I lost all my hap-
piness and peace of mind and I am very disturb about my rela-
tionship with my son

Her son was also disturbed—so disturbed that his struggle to escape her
clutches was the main drama of his life. He had never wanted to go to

medical school—he wanted to be a professional musician and loved to play the piano in speakeasies—but Mama had insisted. He enrolled in Northwestern Medical School and boarded in the Union Theological Seminary on campus; Mama showed up on Sunday nights with a home-cooked dinner covered in tinfoil. After he was married, she would call him up at the office and weep over the phone: Why had he abandoned his mother? Why didn't he invite her over for dinner on Sunday night? But he did, every other Sunday; she alternated with my mother's mother, Grandma Liz, who couldn't stand to be in the same room with her. Grasping, histrionic, shrewd, she had a peasant's canny instinct for making trouble. She played on my father's guilt, tormenting him with accusations of neglect. Is it any wonder that his favorite novel was *Crime and Punishment*?

There was pressure from the other side of the family, too. Grandma Liz was more refined than Raya, and made no effort to hide the fact. She was from a higher class, more educated, more at home in the world. Or so she believed. As I think back on it now, it's quite clear how Liz—*Leezitchka*, we called her—arrived at this conviction of superiority. Wasn't she also an immigrant child from the Old World? But she carried herself with a regal air and draped around herself shawls as brightly colored as a peacock's plumage. Silver bracelets purchased on her trips to Cuernavaca jangled on her thick wrists; her necklace was made of heavy turquoise stones. She moved among a noisy crowd of émigré painters and writers who played pinochle at a card table set up in her Wilmette living room, slapping the cards down and shouting, their billowy white hair shrouded in a cloud of smoke. When the Bolshoi Ballet arrived in town, members of the cast came to drink tea out of tall glasses. The air stank from their gold-tipped black Sobranies.

I close Grandma Raya's notebook and turn to the pile of documents that I've shaken out of the envelope and dumped on the carpet in our living room. Here's Leezitchka's death certificate: "At rest Oct. 15, 1978"—a haunting phrase. The arduous journey is done. She's finally at rest. My grandpa Sam's death certificate is next: age 65. Occupation: executive. He came over on the boat from Russia and started out selling postcards—"pos'l cards," he called them—from a battered suitcase. Sam had an entrepreneurial gift and prospered in the wool business; on my wall is a photograph of him sitting at the wheel of a convertible Duesenberg roadster, looking very pleased with himself. Every morning at eight o'clock "sharp," he called his broker to find out how his investments were doing. "Sol? Sam," he would announce, pacing up and down in the kitchen, a cigarette gripped underhanded in the Russian manner smoldering in his palm.

Grandma Raya's death certificate is here, too: her last residence was the Carlton House Nursing Home. I remember visiting her there: she was in a wheelchair, mouth agape, fish-white skin hanging in folds from her neck. The room smelled faintly of urine. White hairs sprouted from her chin. It was a warm day, and the bleat of horns on Irving Park Road floated through the window.

I examine documents related to our family plot in Woodlawn Cemetery: "Both you and Nora Atlas, and James Atlas are owners in joint tenancy for 'C' section, block 12, lot 10, no. 12.'" Where's my brother? Isn't he going to die, too? I never knew we had a plot at Woodlawn. Does it still belong to us? It would be comforting to know I had somewhere to go.

Another item: my grandparents' marriage certificate ("Samuel Glassenberg and Miss Lizzie Vaslaw"), issued in 1913, now the color of parchment. On a steamship ticket, his name is "Simche." I learn that he came from Minsk by way of Rotterdam on "about" January 14, 1906. He was born on September 15, 1888. So he was eighteen when he got here. He traveled with Meyer Glassenberg (father) and Jacob Glassenberg (brother). His mother also traveled to America on the S.S. *Rotterdam.* Her name is listed as "Unknown." Too late to find out now. My mother doesn't remember, and there's no one else to ask.

Twelve years after his arrival in America, Sam petitions for "naturalization"—citizenship. On the form are questions: Do you understand the principles of government of the United States? Yes. Do you fully believe in the form of government of the United States? Yes.

Why, six years later, in 1924, does he again file a petition? I don't know, but he gets turned down. It isn't until thirty-two years later, on February 8, 1950, that he gets his certificate. His wife—my grandma Liz—has to wait two years longer.

In the same envelope is Grandma Raya's admission to the School of Pharmacy at Valparaiso University School of Pharmacy in 1921. Her grades, unlike her husband's, are poor: D in alkalid analysis, D in pharmaceutical Latin. She flunked dispensing.

Undeterred, she writes, fourteen years later, to Mr. Clinton P. Bliss, Acting Sup't of Registration. It's a mimeograph-blue copy of a typed letter, in impeccable English (did my father write it?), listing her qualifications in a bid for certification: She had "some apothecary (drug store) experience in Russia prior to coming to the United States in the year 1913." She completed 8⅞ units, which fulfilled the requirements of the Illinois Pharmacy Law of 1917. Her certificate of graduation finally arrives—on December 11, 1961. (I know my father said she was slow in school, but forty years?) After he lost his job as an engineer during the Depression, Grandpa Herman also enrolled in pharmacy school and finished in two years.

Grandma is persistent. She bombards congressmen with letters begging them to grant a visa to her sister, Miss Rochla Ginsburg, resident in Vishny Volotchek. Eventually the Honorable Will R. Wood replies with instructions: Miss Ginsburg should communicate with the

consul in Riga, requesting a visa "for the journey to this country." She
will also need an affidavit showing Grandma's citizenship status. At last
the visa comes through. I know this from a telegram with the letterhead
of the Russian Canadian American Passenger Agency at Teatralny
Proezd 8, Moscow, acknowledging payment to the Cunard Steam Ship
of a ticket for the journey across the Atlantic.

And that's how Rochla got to America and became my great-aunt
Rose, whose face rises up before me as I read: full-cheeked, gray-curled,
eyes that melt with love as she clasps me to her. Age eight or nine, I'm
fascinated by her plump bosomy figure, her fragrant neck where she's
dabbed perfume. I remember the gesture I've seen in my mother as I
watch her at the bathroom mirror getting dressed: the chin raised, the
finger lightly jabbing her porcelain skin.

Here's my parents' marriage license ("To any Person Legally Authorized to Solemnize Marriage"), and here are letters from Dad's mother
to my parents on their honeymoon, written on lined notebook paper. "I
do hope that you and Nora should take in all the joy and fun and pleasure
on your wonderful trip, don't pass anything up," she writes to them in
Honolulu: "I hope and pray that all your life should be a continuation
of beauty and a long-long stretch of happiness, joy and gladness." She
herself sounds happy for once:

> July the 17 we were celebrating Harvey's wedding which took
> place at the Edgewater Beach Hotel. It is a very beautiful place.
> The wedding was a small wedding but a very beautiful. They all
> missed you and Nora. Everybody was very happy and gay at the
> wedding.

Who is Harvey? If the couple who wed that day are still together, they
would be celebrating their sixty-sixth anniversary this year. But they'd

have to do it someplace other than the Edgewater Beach Hotel, which was torn down thirty years ago.

I read, with tears in my eyes, the eulogy for Grandma Raya given by Dad's oldest friend, Jerry:

After a long and full life, Raya Atlas has been gathered to her Fathers and for all of us on this day, the summer sun shines less brightly and there is a little less zest to the sparkle of June.

Her life, however, was like a gay summer day rich in the variegated colors and the tapestry of the goodness of life. She came to this country as a young woman, plunged into a life of work and struggle, labored valiantly with her husband of blessed memory, raised a fine outstanding son and eventually by dint of hard unremitting work and appreciation of life's endearing values emerged into the sunlit spaces of achievement and happiness.

A loving tribute, but this is not how I heard the story. After Grandpa opened the drugstore they operated on the Northwest Side, the couple had little pleasure in life. Grandpa suffered from debilitating depression, according to my father. An envelope entitled "Old Letter" offers a glimpse of their existence. Grandpa is writing to my father, a young physician stationed in the Aleutian Islands during World War II. "Things here are abt the same as usual except for the confounded heat for the last few days made it unbearable to come up to our overheated apartment for meals or sleep." Where did they sleep? Was their apartment over the shop?

It's only a sentence, but enough for me to imagine them sweltering in the heavy summer air, a propeller-size fan hung from the brown pressed-tin ceiling turning lazily in the gloom. When a customer enters, the heat blasts through the door. Grandma and Grandpa sit on metal folding chairs in the back, a pitcher of ice water on a table. The street is empty; nothing stirs. It's not the life they wanted.

My mother's birth certificate, signed by Richard J. Daley, then the county clerk—his dynastic rule as mayor of Chicago still a few decades off. My footprint; Dad's military record ("Victory Medal," "American Theater Service Medal"); his diploma from Northwestern University School of Medicine; a brochure for a lecture he gave on reversible renal insufficiency. His birth certificate: 8/31/13. Beside the category "Race or color (if not of the white race)," he is listed as "Hebrew." But what's this? Why is Donald named as David? On the facing page of the photostat is a second document, labeled Affidavit and Certificate of Correction. "David" should be changed to "Donald." The date affixed to this document is 8/31/1951. How strange that he began life with a different name and I never knew about it. And why did he wait thirty-eight years to change it?

I unfold a three-page statement, single spaced, from my father to the House Un-American Activities Committee, giving an account of his life and concluding with an assertion of his innocence: "At no time have I ever contributed financially to, been sympathetic with or been a member of any organization listed as subversive by the Attorney General of the United States." But he holds his ground with dignity. As a Jew, he declares, he is "violently opposed to fascism as well as communism, for fascism can only bring a repetition of the destruction of 6,000,000 Jews of World War II." On July 15, 1955, a letter arrives from the Veterans Administration Hospital: "Our Central Office has informed us that your employment is clearly consistent with the interests of the national security and a certificate of security clearance has been placed in your personnel folder." The bureaucratic language muffles the terror that McCarthy's vicious witch hunt must have inspired in a young Jewish doctor trying to make his way in what was then a WASP-dominated profession—less than a decade after the Holocaust. I sit cross-legged in front of the TV set, wondering why my father is transfixed by the hectoring, ill-shaven, puffy-faced man yelling in the grainy black-and-white film jittering on the screen.

A bundle of photographs: Grandma Raya in her tasseled mortarboard and gown, also beaming, her face wreathed in a puff of black curls. Liz and Sam's bohemian circle. They sit in languid poses; one handsome young man in the foreground has slipped his hand between the buttons of his jacket like Napoleon. It's 1925 or so. How do I know this? Because there's a demure little girl in the picture, in a white dress: my mother. She's instantly recognizable, even though it was eighty years ago. *Famous auto trip around Lake Michigan with Jerry, Marty Witkin and Donald 1935.* The boys are in bathing suits on a pier; Jerry, hands clasped, is about to dive into the lake. Marty is grasping Jerry's hands as if to prevent him while Donald pretends he's about to whack him with an oar. The boys are smiling, having fun.

In their own minds, at that moment, they're deep in their own lives. The "famous" auto trip is in fact famous in their own minds—it's a defining event for them, part of the family lore. We think of ourselves not as located in a continuum, part of an ever-evolving world, but as its endpoint. All of human history has been leading up to us. It's hard—impossible—to grasp that we, too, will seem quaint to the generations that follow us, our clothes strange, our images fixed in a remote moment in time.

I've been reading for hours. Dusk has fallen, and the room is nearly dark. I gather up the papers, put them back in the manila envelope, and stow them in the cupboard.

I sit on the couch next to the coffee table where our family albums are piled up. The photos are arranged in chronological order. We're in our twenties, when it was just the two of us, standing beside our bicycles in

Vermont. I have so much hair! We're thin, dressed in Windbreakers, jeans, and heavy lace-up shoes, smiling shyly at the camera. I can't remember who took the picture. Hiking in the Lake District in bulky pullovers, knapsacks strapped to our backs. Our wedding, the children in our future nonexistent—the pre-Molly, pre-William world.

An album later, they arrive. First the girl, wrapped in a pink blanket, her dark hair spiky, her eyes wide open; then the boy, bald-headed and Buddha-faced. As we turn the pages, the little children crouching over a fish pond or prancing on the lawn in their pajamas become bigger children, waving tennis rackets, swinging baseball bats, driving go-karts, jumping into a pool. For a few years, there are lots of Halloween photos—a bumblebee, a pirate, a ballerina. Then—boom!—they're off to camp, boarding yellow school buses. They sit on bleachers for their class portraits: kindergarten, first grade, second grade, third . . . and—wait a second—don't tell me they're graduating! Molly's in a white dress, Will's in a blue blazer. The widowed grandmothers are there. Anna and I hover in the background, smiling weakly, proud, baffled—irrelevant.

And here are the kids in their bulky parkas and white podlike helmets, craggy snowcapped mountains in the background. We're smiling, leaning jauntily on our poles. It all comes back to me: the sharp, blustery air at the top when you push off the lift chair and swoop down the steep incline, skating off to the side, fiddling with your fogged-up goggles, smartly pulling your gloves tight, stamping to shake the snow from your skis, heading off toward the slope on the powdery trail, your breath puffing out, then halting at the brink, skis pointing just over the edge, to admire the view—the skiers flying down the slope, the gondola suspended on its taut cable, the forested mountains in the distance, the lodge nestled in the valley far below, and, with a deep intake of breath, pushing off and making your first sharp turn. The bright sun makes the white snow whiter. My breath plumes in the clear crisp air.

Beside the photograph of us on the mountain is another, taken a year later. I'm wearing corduroys, not ski pants, hiking shoes instead of ski boots. I won't be skiing today; in fact, I won't be skiing ever again. The year I turned fifty I skidded off the trail in Vermont, hurtled into the forest, and smashed against a tree. My arm was shattered; it took seven strong men to lift me onto a stretcher and get me down the slope, towed by a ski-mobile. I had nerve damage in addition to a broken arm; for seven months the question of whether my hand would ever work again hung in the balance. After two operations and a "tendon transfer," I've regained most of the use of my fingers. The pins in my shoulder set off the alarm at airport security. So that's it: I can't take a chance on another spill.

I remember the morning that picture was taken. Anna snapped it on a disposable camera in the parking lot. She wasn't skiing, either; she found the labor of getting up on the mountain—the equipment, the lines, the chaos in the cafeteria—not worth the effort. She preferred hanging around the lodge now or hiking in the woods. I clipped the kids' ski passes onto their parkas, fumbling with my damaged fingers in the cold, waved good-bye, and slid behind the steering wheel of the van. Together we sat looking out the windshield as they glided over to the lift for the first run of the day, and drove back to the hotel to read our books by the fire.

I linger over a sequence of photographs from when the children went to a summer camp in the Berkshires. It wasn't a regular camp: no baseball diamond, no tennis courts, no lake, and no canoes. The owners, a couple from Boston who had fled their oppressive Brahmin families to live the rural life, loved art and music and theater. The main event was a Shakespeare play that was staged at the end of each summer. Jed and Sarah poured their hearts into the production, designing sets and costumes, putting the campers through long hours of rehearsal. In the barn, they transformed themselves into jugglers, jesters, soldiers, princes in tights fashioned out of ladies' hose from Wal-Mart. In the photographs, the crowd of actors in full dress is marching down the hill to the glade. And here's a photo that shows the zipline strung between two giant elms; Will is about to land on the stage in Elizabethan curl-toe booties. What play was that? *A Midsummer Night's Dream*? And here's Molly as Macbeth—men played women's parts in those days; why couldn't women play men's? Her long tresses bundled up beneath a velvet hood, she's brandishing a wooden sword at Macduff—Max Sussman.

The camp shut down a few years ago. The couple is divorced, their money is gone—some financial catastrophe in the family. Jed works at the local Blockbuster; Sarah teaches drawing at an art school. The property has been sold. Only the snapshots are left.

I think of the children's children leafing through our album and coming across these photographs. They'll puzzle over the scene, trying to match their ancestors with the children's faces. Is that Mom in the hood? And that must be Will, aged ten or so, in a flowing black robe, holding a book open—the priest in *Twelfth Night* who marries Viola to the Duke. See those arched eyebrows and that handsome blade of a nose? He looks a little like . . . Ben, Ted, Bernard? Some child as yet unborn.

Already our photographs are showing their age, the edges yellowing, the crisp bright color beginning to fade.

Home

It's nearly midnight when we pull into the driveway of our farmhouse in Vermont. We've come up for the weekend, and it's been a long drive from New York— three hours and twenty-seven minutes. I like to compute how long it takes, noting the time on the dashboard clock when we leave the city and the time when we arrive. Tonight we left at 8:07, and it's now 11:34. Good, but not even close to our best time. Three years ago we made it in three hours and twelve minutes—though I nearly killed us on the last stretch, a dirt road that veers sharply rightward a few hundred yards from the house. "Are you *crazy*?" Anna shouted as we skidded around the turn. "We're at 3:11, three minutes ahead of the record," I explained, as if accelerating on a dirt country road in the dark of night was the most reasonable thing in the world, like driving to Price Chopper. On another occasion, I was ahead of our best time as we barreled along the Taconic; just before the turnoff to Route 22, I heard the siren and spotted the rotating red light. Shit. I pulled over and waited for the state trooper's shadow to fill my window. "Did you know you were going seventy-eight in a fifty-mile-an-hour zone?" "No, I didn't, sir." "Trust me. I've got it right here on my radar gun." He flourished it at me like the Light Saber of a Jedi in *Star Wars*. It took him twenty minutes to write out the ticket: $175. The family always laughs at my contention that "it would have been our best time if I hadn't been caught speeding."

We've made the drive so many hundreds of times over the last three decades that my body and brain have internalized it. I know every bend in the road, every gas station and house; I know to the minute when the sign that says COLUMBIA COUNTY will appear out of the dark, and when, eighteen minutes later, the red-lettered neon sign—*DINER*—will loom up out of the mist. I feel a surge of joy as we pull into the parking lot, anticipating the cup of stale coffee and the dusty flavorless doughnut that await me (provided I'm not trying tó beat the 3:12-minute record). Hanging over the door is a banner that says ORIGINAL OWNER BACK. It's been there for three years.

Finally the house appears in our headlights. I speed up once more, involuntarily, gunning the accelerator. This time no one complains. We're all eager to get there, to hear the crunch of tires on the gravel driveway. What's the hurry? It's that we're coming home. To be honest, it's a second home. Our primary residence—as it's described in tax documents and mortgage applications—is in Manhattan. But the Vermont house feels as much like home as our apartment on the Upper West Side does when we fumble for our keys in the elevator and push open the front door. For people in our situation—New Yorkers of what George Orwell called "the lower upper middle-class"—professors, psychiatrists, writers, editors—the claustrophobic, high-pressure atmosphere of New York makes having a second home in the country a high priority, even if you have to take out a whopping mortgage or work twelve-hour days to pay for it.

The homes my friends and I have bought—or in our case, inherited—were bought on a shoestring, money eked out over years of scrimping and saving. They didn't look in the Hamptons or the Berk-shires; they looked in Ulster County and Columbia County, where real estate was cheap. They snapped up wrecks, farmhouses that were liter-ally falling down. They searched the pages of local papers, combed through listings supplied by Upstate real estate agents who drove old cars and wore threadbare sports jackets. "This isn't for a few years; this is for life," said one of our friends, reporting a conversation he'd had with his wife, who was reluctant to pour money into a house in Ancram that hadn't been occupied for years and had a family of badgers living in the kitchen.

Why was this house-hunt and house-fixing-up phase of our lives so consuming? Why did so many people I know spend their weekends speeding over the back roads and slowing down whenever they saw a FOR SALE sign in front of a house? Why did I hunger on muggy summer Friday nights to gun our rental car over the bridge out of Manhattan as the setting sun kindled the George Washington Bridge into a blazing arc of light, the children in the backseat off in Walkmanland while Anna and I listened to *Rigoletto*? Was it a love of nature, the crisp northern air clearing our lungs, the crickets chirping in the fields? Or was it that and something more—a longing for the innocent long-ago time when we had no grown-up responsibilities—no jobs, no children (beloved as they are), no bills to pay, no deaths in the family, none of the losses that are starting to add up. As I pad across the dew-perfumed lawn in bare feet—it's early in the morning the night after our long drive up from the city—I try to clear my head of city woes and remember what it was like not to worry all the time. The title of a Keats sonnet, long buried in the college English course file lodged somewhere in my brain, emerges into the sunlight: "To one who has been long in city pent." That's it: that's what I'm feeling. *Pent.*

Sometimes I picture us all from above, as if from a satellite hovering

over the earth, dispersing through the black countryside like moles bur-
rowing in their tunnels, heading with blind instinctual determination
toward the refuge of home. Once I saw a picture in the Metropolitan
Museum by Sanford Gifford, a painter of the Hudson River School: in
the forefront is a clearing, stumps of trees still raw in the freshly tilled
earth. The weather is wintry, the sky striated with pink-tinted clouds in
the darkening afternoon. In the background is a house, hardly more
than a cabin, its windows ablaze with light. I stared at the picture for a
long time, haunted by those two orange squares glowing in the dusk—a
stay, however illusory, against the cold, encroaching dark.

After the long drive up to Vermont, we get out of the car. The
engine ticks in the silence. A deer stands motionless in the field, caught
in our headlights. Fireflies wink in the mist that billows over the lawn
like steam from an open manhole cover. I stand in the driveway, inhaling the damp, loamy scent of fresh-cut grass. I can hear the faint swish
of cars out on Route 67A. It used to bother me, but it doesn't anymore.
I'm home.

Our house resembles our friends' houses—cottages or farmhouses built
by real settlers, homesteaders, pilgrims from England or their ancestors
who cleared the forests tree by tree and stone by stone—a time unimag-
inably distant from our own soft era. In the summer, Revolutionary
War reenacters set up camp in a field down the road and stand in
clumps on a knoll, rifles at the ready, picking one another off in a puff
of smoke with erratic bursts of gunfire. Every once in a while a redcoat
or a rebel dressed in leatherskin breaches topples to the ground. The
question that nags at me is this: How did the two sides even find each
other to engage? Didn't they wander around the countryside in total
confusion, trudging for miles through muddy fields in search of the
enemy?

When our house was built, the trip up from New York would have taken two days by stagecoach, with a stop in Albany to change horses. But the house itself is pretty much as it was. Will, put off by the rough-hewn floorboards, the preindustrial flathead nails that shred his tennis socks, above all the lack of a television set, refers to it as "geezer house." It *is* pretty old—two hundred years, estimates our contractor, Craig, who makes improvements on the house as we can afford them. Craig's guess is that it was built out of wood retrieved from a barn, and that the farmer who originally lived in it had to struggle to eke out a living from the field we now own. How hard that life must have been! No cars, no electricity, no cell phones to gab away on while lying in a hammock. There wasn't even a fireplace; a few years ago, we put one in ourselves. They must have managed with just a hearth—long since walled up somewhere in the front of the house when it was just four rooms, two up and two down.

Houses, like people, evolve over time, transforming themselves, mutating into different identities. Our house evolved in tandem with the increase in our disposable income, from a ramshackle dwelling that we shared with Anna's brother, Tom, in the 1970s to the modest but gentrified home it is today—charming, we think, to those with rural, garden-conscious sensibilities, readers of seed catalogs and *Country Living*. Anna's mother bought it in 1974 for $27,000, which in those days— the phrase, tinged with hoary nostalgia, begins to recur as one grows older—seemed like a lot of money. The previous owner, a woman who lived there for seventy years, was in the habit of throwing cans out in the yard. The dirt-floor cellar was piled high with yellowing newspapers. The shed out back was falling down. The neighbors' dogs barked all night. On old maps, the area around our house was labeled Sodom.

Over the next few years, Anna's brother and his wife lived there full-time. Tom and Tully were 1960s folk, admirably unmaterialistic. They drove a rust-mottled VW bus and sang Pete Seeger songs around the wood-burning stove, accompanying themselves on banjo and guitar. Their idea of a vacation was a month in a Labrador fisherman's shed. They didn't buy into the home-improvement mania; they liked the house the way it was. Tom had bought a tractor and farmed the field; Tully had a big organic garden. They kept chickens that roosted in the trees. Over time, the property took shape.

We came in the summer, usually for a month, and had our own "wing" upstairs, with a bathroom and a rudimentary kitchen: a fridge, a hot plate, a sink. We decorated the walls of our room with Atget photos and bookshelves fashioned from boards and cinder blocks. We were happy. From our window, we could see the river that meandered through the property, silver in the summer sunlight, a dull tarnish when it rained. We didn't have a car; I would pedal my bicycle to the farmers' market in the next town over and fill up a knapsack with groceries. We blistered our soft city hands scything the edges of the lawn, bent over like Millais's gleaners.

When we leaf through our photo album now, the decrepitude of the house in those days (again, the carbon-dating phrase) is unsettling. Cotton tufts of stuffing sprouted like cauliflower from the couch. Fly-paper hung from the kitchen ceiling. The banks of the river were strewn with tires and oil drums. The propane tank around the side of the house inclined like the Leaning Tower of Pisa. How could we have lived like that? The answer is: we were young.

I liked the town. Even by Vermont standards, it was small. The center consisted of five buildings: a white-pillared country store built in the early 1800s; a restaurant; a redbrick library; and Percy's, a general store out of another era if not another century. It had a magazine rack with sun-discolored comic books and out-of-date hot-rod magazines; an ancient fan with prop propeller-size blades that hung from the pressed-tin ceiling; a marble soda counter with chrome spigots and red vinyl-seated stools that reminded me of my grandpa Herman's drugstore in Chicago. It reeked of stale cat piss; my brother, visiting one weekend, stumbled out holding a handkerchief to his face as if he'd been tear-gassed. Mrs. Percy, who was born in the Victorian age and looked it in her high lace-up boots, sat behind the counter, nodding off over the cash register. Her son, Junior, ran the taxi service, driving a dusty black limousine that had been passed down from the town's rich family, the McCulloughs, who had once inhabited the Victorian mansion up the road from our house; it was a museum now. On Saturday nights before we owned a car, we would hire Junior to drive us to the movie theater in the local mall, where he would sit and wait for us in the parking lot with his friend, a saturnine mechanic named Tex.

The area was hardly picturesque. There were no zoning laws to speak of; the road from our town to the next town over was lined with filling stations, gun shops, McDonald's, a Best Western, a dairy bar, a Chinese restaurant called Hot Woks. (We brought home an order of ribs once and were so alarmed by their raw pinkish hue that we drove them to the Dumpster behind the local convenience store and tossed the foil-lined bag in like a grenade.) I bought socks and tennis balls at Wal-Mart.

There wasn't much to do. The bowling alley closed at nine o'clock. You'd go into the SevenPlex and watch a first-run movie with four other people in the theater. But I liked it, liked the miniature golf course and the go-kart track, the country club where the cracked-asphalt tennis courts, their seams bursting with crabgrass, served as a parking lot for golf carts. Sometimes if you called up Gimme Pizza you got a busy signal for an hour because the guy who worked the ovens had run out of dough and taken the phone off the hook. By the entrance to the Stop & Shop was a game called Skil-Klaw: you fed a quarter into the machine and a metal clamp zoomed out over a clump of stuffed animals; you had thirty seconds to maneuver it downward and try to snag one. Will and I played this game until our last quarter was gone. When he wasn't there, I sheepishly played alone, as furtive as a gambler at a slot machine. Tooling around town, I felt a peace of mind that I rarely felt in New York. I gorged on beef jerky and Hostess Baseballs. I was free.

Like many urban dwellers drawn to the country life, I tended to sentimentalize my relationship with the locals. I was gratified by the most perfunctory exchange. When Butch, the farmer who tilled the field, stood beside me on the front steps gazing out over the land, a filterless Camel cupped underhand in his palm, I would savor our nearly wordless communion. "Whatcha gonna put in this year?" I'd say in my weekender's country drawl, a railroad cap on my head and a long blade of grass between my teeth. "Corn." I nodded sagely: Corn. Good choice. "We'll raid the field and pick some for ourselves," I said. "That's *cow corn*, Jim," Butch replied.

At the country store in town, I didn't have to pay cash like the people from Connecticut or New York just passing through; not me. I kept a "tab," the privilege of customers on a first-name basis with Larry, the white-haired, white-aproned proprietor whose father had owned the store before him. Why did I find such gratification in this familiarity with tradesmen? Why was I suffused with gratitude when I came in for some lamb chops and the butcher, Mr. Mickle, called me "Jim"? For the same reason that I experienced a mild frisson of pleasure whenever I opened a utility bill and saw the address: Little Red House on Harrington Road. There was an element of Romantic pastoral in this celebration of country life—the classic longing for rural innocence, an escape from the corrupt city to the idyllic provinces. But it also provided a sense of permanence, of place, of connection with the past. "The road to my house has not changed in two hundred years," writes David Mamet in his book on Vermont, "and in one hundred, in fifty years perhaps, the dirt road will be paved, the paved road will be lined with homes, the bear, wolf, fox, moose, mountain lion will be gone, as the woods will be gone." But the house will still be there.

After a decade, Tom moved into town and embarked on a career as a museum curator. The place was ours. We rolled up our sleeves and got to work, yuppifying in earnest. We spent hours at the local interior decorating shop pulling down huge books filled with samples and brought home scraps to pin on the wall. I could finally sympathize with the plaintive cry of a friend in the throes of renovation: "I'm having a wallpaper meltdown." It was embarrassing to find ourselves sitting around the dinner table with friends and going on about faucets, debating the merits of Kohler and Miele. Late at night, we sat side by side glued to the computer, trolling the Internet for doorknobs.

We poured gravel on the driveway, until then a muddy trough. Our landscaper friends, a gay couple named Joe and Wayne who had been early settlers in Vermont, put in a garden with a stone terrace. We built a deck out by the river. We didn't have an architect: Anna cut out photographs from shelter magazines—*House & Garden, American Home*—and books with titles like *Shabby Chic*.

We bought a bed. We had, through the half-century mark of our existence on this earth, been sleeping—in the country, anyway—on a double mattress with a metal frame from The Mattress King, a retail outlet in a strip mall a few miles outside of town. Ordered from a Pottery Barn catalog, our bed arrived by way of a delivery truck so huge that its top pushed aside the branches of trees on both sides of the road. Anna was in New York, and as I wrestled the headboard and sideboards out of their cardboard containers, I was alarmed to note what looked like a badly botched paint job. "It's scarred and scuffed all over," I reported. "Another two-errand errand." The phrase was a coinage of ours employed to describe a peculiar phenomenon we'd noticed over the years: not even the simplest chore is ever accomplished on the first try; it requires a trial run in which the thing is first done wrong. Anna laughed. "It's distressed." My mind scrambled to make sense of the inanimate pronoun. "Distressed?" *I* was distressed. Only then was the interior-decorating term for artificially treating a piece of furniture to make it look old explained to me. Our antique bed came fresh from the factory.

We rent the house for nine months of the year to pay the property taxes. On Memorial Day weekend we drive up after the tenants move out and unpack our belongings from a locked room. The house is like an empty stage, our possessions the props; the drama of summer in the country is about to unfold. Once the furniture has been installed, we turn to the business of putting out our things: the photographs and lamps, the china, the wooden candlesticks and brass teakettle we bought at a yard sale in Hoosick Falls. There's stuff I hardly remember we own: a miniature bookshelf from Venice, crammed with tiny scrolls and tiny leather-bound books; a stuffed squirrel with a walnut clamped between its jaws. There are watercolors of the dirt road with its bower of trees, of the falling-down shed built by Tom years ago. And here are the porcelain rooster salt-and-pepper shakers from God knows where. There's a Corps of Engineers map of the area that shows our actual house, a square black speck beside the Walloomsac River. Wherein lies the power of these objects? They serve to customize our home, to give it the particularity that signifies: this is ours.

Our work of reclamation done, I float through the sun-filled rooms, plumping myself down first in the living-room easy chair, then on the sofa, then on the back-porch rocker, taking in the house from different angles. Its imperfections—the cracked window, the picket fence with missing slats, the shed door with a loose hinge—don't bother me; they mirror our own imperfections. A house reveals more than the taste of its inhabitants; it's the visible expression of their character traits. Our house is eccentric, old-fashioned, plain, put together in a haphazard way that struggles toward a coherent identity. It reflects back to us who we are, or at least who we'd like to be.

The place is starting at last to acquire that lived-in look we've been admiring in catalogs and magazines for so many years. Anna likes to say the house is a "duck-rabbit"—the silhouetted image that, if you look at it from one angle, is a duck and from another angle a rabbit. When it's a duck, it's a sweet, comfortable house; when it's a rabbit, it's a dump. Driving up in the middle of winter to drop off a case of books on our way up to ski, we're demoralized by its bleakness. The branches of the leafless trees whip forlornly in the wind, and the neighbors' houses stand out against the sky. Inside, the tenants' furniture that has displaced our own, stored away in a back room, makes the house seem somehow less ours. Our footsteps echo on the rugless floors.

It is what it is. We've made our nest. Its modesty sometimes makes me a little wistful, but to see the things we've accumulated over a lifetime all in their place is reassuring. Today the house is a duck.

I am putting up a picture in the living room. We paid twelve quid for it at a print shop near the British Museum and had it framed. This is how we collect most of the art on our walls: buying old prints cheap and framing them nicely to give them new life. We have a lithograph of an English country house set among verdant sheep-dotted fields, and another of an Oxford college. The one I'm putting up now, on a hot August day, bees buzzing around their hive by the side door, is a lithograph of a nineteenth-century square in London, Middle Row Holborn. I love to contemplate this picture—the tall house at the center, smoke pouring from the chimneys on the roof, the cobblestone street crowded with carriages, men and women strolling beneath streetlamps in their quaint garb—top hats for the men, ankle-length dresses for the women. I make up a story in my head about the scene: life went at a stately pace in those days, social status was fixed. People lived in one place and put down roots.

Like most stories—all stories?—this one is pure invention. The London I contemplate in the picture was as transient then as the world I inhabit now. I have been to Middle Row Holborn, and the old buildings are jumbled in with bleak modern offices. So why do I imbue the scene in my little print with an aura of permanence and order that it couldn't possibly have possessed? What is the appeal of these quaint pictures on my wall with their houses that have actual names: The Old Priory, Admington Hall, Boar's Hill Lodge? They unlock a longing to have lived other lives in other places and other times; but there's some deeper feeling, too. In my imagination, they represent an escape from the relentless struggle Americans must engage in to create their own identities. Each generation has to begin all over again; except for maybe the *Mayflower* upper crust with its New England homes passed on from one member of the family to the next, or farmers who tenaciously possess their land, we're migrants, restlessly moving, changing jobs, tearing up our roots. I hear that the people upstairs, after two years of strenuous renovation, have put their apartment on the market. "You're moving?" I say to my neighbor in the elevator. "We needed another room," he explains—and so the process of buying an apartment and selling the one he's got, getting a bridge loan, picking out paint, buying new bathroom fixtures, installing, rewiring, putting up and taking down, begins anew, an endless cycle of relocation.

I'm trying to emulate my ideal home, the one I found depicted in a big coffee-table book called *Scottish Country*. It has old stone fireplaces, worn Persian rugs, lots of bookshelves, a mud room with rows of

Wellington boots leaned up against the tongue-in-groove wainscoting. In the low-ceilinged sitting room with rough-hewn beams, the maroon walls are covered with framed pictures. These rooms, with their encrustations, like geologic strata, of possessions acquired over generations, represent historical continuity. The English tend to inhabit their homes as the tenants of their epoch, stewards of property that has long preceded them and will long outlast them; they don't have to scavenge for stuff to fill the empty rooms, then sell it off at an open house or consign it to the local antiques dealer when it's time to close up shop. When I study the offerings in the window of our local real estate office, I'm disheartened by their provisional, temporary air, each living room furnished in a nearly identical style—the chilly bare floors, glass-topped coffee tables, leather couches, cheap chandeliers. Why do people even bother to move their furniture? Since it's so interchangeable, why not just leave it all for the next occupant?

The first time I visited my parents at their retirement home in California, I was oppressed by how barren it was. The house was a stucco split-level, in a subdivision of nearly identical split-levels; it was only a few years old, and the vegetation was sparse. It was perched on a vine-covered knoll, and the patio looked out over the desert, where coyotes howled at night. I resisted the place, and took the family there as seldom as possible. After a decade, I still hadn't learned how to navigate the five-minute drive from their house to downtown. But gradually I grew to love it, especially after the children were born. They played on the beach, watched seals cavort in a cove, rode the roller coaster in the amusement park on the boardwalk in San Diego. The plants and shrubs around the house began to flourish. The desert grew dense with houses and shopping centers. My parents made improvements, found new friends, planted a garden of spiky desert shrubs. After they'd been there for thirty years, La Jolla, too, was home—just in time for them to pack up and leave.

All across the country, the same ritual is being enacted: the packing up of a lifetime's worth of *tchotchkes,* the sifting of photographs, the dispersal of artwork and silverware to children, the house put on the market and sold to a younger couple with kids. Pretty soon it will be our turn to begin divesting ourselves of our possessions, going through the albums, pruning the books. Our home-size grows and shrinks the way our body mass grows and shrinks. You go from the little house to the bigger house to the still bigger house, then downsize to a smaller house, then a still smaller house until you're crammed back into a single room. Then the smallest room of all—the narrow, wooden, rectangular one, with the handles.

And so I'm taking my stand against transience, digging in my heels like a homesteader with his rifle defending the piece of land he's hewn out of the forest. I won't move or be moved. I have my paraphernalia: hammer, hook, tape measure, Scotch tape to put over where I'm going to bang in the nail so that it doesn't shatter the plaster, pencil to mark the place where I'm going to put in the nail. The Middle Row Holborn picture goes above the English country house and the Oxford college— or should it go below? The frame is nice, a plain brown wood border.

I decide to put the new picture above the other two. The thing is, it's very hard to get it centered. It has to be two inches above the one below it, because that's the distance between that one and the one below *it.* Then I have to measure the distance between the top of the wire and the frame, and subtract that—or do I add it?—to the two inches. So it's 2 inches plus $1\frac{5}{8}$ of an inch . . . I'm sweating by now, balancing on the second step of the ladder I've dragged out of the closet. I remove the nail from between my lips, fit it through the hook, and hammer it in where I've put a mark. I hang the picture on the hook and stand back to survey my handiwork. No! It's at least three inches above the other one. I take it down and pull out the nail with the hammer claw, but somehow I pull too hard and bend the nail. I go into the kitchen, open the tool drawer, and rifle through the contents—string, batteries, screwdrivers, window shade pulls, a wrench, a miniature flashlight, a loop of twine—in search of another hook and nail. None to be found.

I can't stop now. I scoop the car keys out of the ceramic bowl on the sill, grab my Yankees cap, and head out to the car. Speeding to Aubuchon hardware store in the mall, I think: isn't it a little strange to be going through all this labor, two hours by now, of hanging a five-by-seven-inch picture of no value on the living room wall of a three-bedroom farmhouse in Vermont? But I'm obsessed: maybe if I get this one thing right, it will feel as if the house is complete. Home is in the details.

At Aubuchon, I buy several packets of picture hooks in different sizes to forestall a two-errand errand. I drive back home at inadvisable speed, whomping over the rutted mud, eager to "close"—to get the deal done. This time it goes without a hitch: the pencil dot has been a bull's-eye; the measurements are right; the nail goes in; the plaster beneath its strip of Scotch tape doesn't crumble or crack. *This is it,* I think as I step back again. Perfect! Here the picture has been hung and here the picture will stay. The three pictures stacked up on the wall beside the fireplace make the room look cozy, *stuffed*—a little bit like the room in *Scottish Country.* Never mind that we've only been here for a single generation; even the retired auto mechanic across the road has occupied his house longer. It's a start.

I've always been fascinated by obits where it says that the deceased "had homes in" New York and Woodstock, Massachusetts, or Boston and Blue Hill, Maine. It wasn't just that the person had the good fortune to own two houses; I want to know what kind of houses. Was the one in the country a pre-Revolutionary farmhouse? A green-shuttered white-clapboard two-story colonial? A gray-shingled house on a bay? It seems like such a graceful way to die: in your own house, stretched out on a high bed with a view from your window of a boat-cluttered harbor.

Lying in a hammock, I compose my obit for the local paper: . . . *died at his home in Manhattan . . . survived by his wife and two children . . . author of . . . worked for . . . had a home in North Bennington, Vermont.*

That last part comforts me.

Money

It's after midnight, and I'm seated at my desk in the corner of our living room—my "study"—sorting through a stack of bills. I have a method for this end-of-the-month ritual: pay the small ones—phone, Con Ed, the cable company—first; then the larger, three-figure bills—bank loan, miscellaneous doctors, telephones (between cell phones and AOL lines, an ever-proliferating number); finally, the whoppers, the budget busters: maintenance (*gotta pay that one*), mortgage, tuition. Lastly—take a deep breath—the credit cards: MasterCard, Visa, American Express. When I open the envelopes, I'm as nervous as a presenter at the Academy Awards; my hand literally trembles. Impossible to predict the new monthly charges: stuff shows up that I completely forgot about. Restaurants, rental cars, Barnes & Noble, tennis lessons; and what is this "cash allowance" charge on one of my credit cards? It must have been the day I exceeded my overdraft—the ATM was stonewalling—and I had to get a loan from Visa at a bank teller's window. Add to this staggering deficit the previous month's balance and you have a figure that induces a fluttering sensation in the pit of the stomach—I'm definitely on Queasy Street. I consult the "minimum balance owed"—always a reassuringly small amount; they want to keep you in debt, let those interest charges mount. $123.47. Fine. I'll pay that.

The other big-ticket expenses I put back neatly in the drawer. The fact that there are only two of these is pleasing; look how many bills I've paid, I think, eyeing the tall stack. Never mind that the ones I haven't paid add up to thousands of dollars, while the ones I *have* paid add up to a few hundred. There's a tidiness to the enterprise, a sense of having put my life in order. As for the accrued debt, I always think of something the editor and social critic Irving Kristol, a guru of an older generation, once said to me: "Just work at what you think is important; the money will follow." Remarkably enough, this seems to be the case. There is never enough—by the time I've finished adding up my income for the month on the calculator, and then subtracted the monies paid out, I'm once again in the red. Yet we somehow manage to keep our little ship afloat. Unlike Dr. Johnson, who had to endure bailiffs camping out in his parlor, or Dickens's father, who was carted off to debtors' prison, I'm permitted to proceed unencumbered with my daily life, getting and spending, adding to my collection of credit cards, piling up debt. It's the American way.

What amazes me is how little this ritual has changed over the years. Rumor has it that a tremendous boom occurred on Wall Street in the 1990s. The stock market soared; Silicon Valley produced hordes of millionaires—along with an impressive roster of billionaires, whatever those are. Whole sectors of the population became rich overnight. There was a speculative fever abroad in the land. Even my most bookish friends began to talk of their "portfolios." Meanwhile, we sat in the conference room of an investment firm on Seventh Avenue and listened to a mild-mannered man in a gray suit explain to us why our money was growing at the rate of 1.2 percent a year. ("The market is off.")

Gray Suit wasn't our first choice as an investment counselor. Not long after we moved to New York, in the late 1970s, I had called upon a senior partner at one of the old-line firms who had been referred to me by a friend of Anna's stepfather. His office was stunning: on the forty-seventh floor of a Third Avenue skyscraper, it had floor-to-ceiling windows that looked all the way down to the prow of Manhattan, with its forest of towers (the two tallest sadly gone now) embraced by the Hudson and the East Rivers, traversed by tugs and barges leaving white Vs in their wake. Far below was a dizzying grid of streets; the north-south avenues in their narrow canyons were filled with yellow taxis, the streetlights turning from green to red and back like a string of colored beads. The partner sat behind an empty desk the size of a Ping-Pong table. He had on a dark suit and wore thick black-rimmed glasses; his cheeks had the ruddy, veinous hue of the rich.

Our interview was awkward and brief. Anna and I were just starting out in the workforce; our nest egg, such as it was, couldn't have remotely approached six figures. "I don't take on clients whose net worth is less than half a million," our prospective investment counselor said. But he was interested in the fact that I was a writer. "I'm writing a memoir," he said brightly. "It's been kind of a hobby of mine." He had grown up on Park Avenue in the 1920s in a formal household—his father had been a successful dry-goods merchant—and he was writing about that distant era, when "people of means," as he described his family, had servants, drank a pitcher of martinis before dinner, and were driven to school in chauffeured limousines. "It's a world that's disappeared and ought to be preserved," he said, the tips of his fingers pressed steeplelike together. Would I care to read it?

I descended in the swift, silent elevator armed with a bulky manuscript in a binder. (It turned out to be lousy, I'm glad to say.)

The visit wasn't a total loss. Perhaps feeling a twinge of pity, Anna's stepfather's friend's associate had given me the name of a broker at another firm who might be willing to take us on. Thus it was that we came under the fiduciary supervision of Gray Suit. Not only did he agree to manage our assets, but he also lavished insane amounts of time and attention on us, considering our modest account. You could always get him on the phone, and he seemed willing to go over the numbers—how much was in mutual funds, how much in bonds, how much in "equities," a term I scarcely understood—in his droning, methodical way for half an hour in the middle of the day. I found his accessibility worrisome: how much can this guy possibly be making on us? Yet Gray Suit himself was obviously well-off. At one meeting, he described the lavish bar mitzvah he was planning for his son out on Long Island: the tent, the party bags, the Peter Duchin band, the catered sit-down dinner for two hundred. I was really beginning to harbor a strong suspicion that you didn't have to be the sharpest tool in the shed (if I may mix my metaphors) to make your nut.

There was no "trickle-down effect." Our unreadable monthly statements, page upon page of indecipherable numbers—"custodial positions," "margined policy," "liquid asset fund"—added up to a profit of three figures. It amazed me to contemplate the firm's employees engaged in diligently toting up these numbers; how did they cover their overhead? In the windowless boardroom. I tried to focus on the difference between corporate fixed income and government securities, but the fact is I simply didn't care. What I wanted to know was how much money I had, and whether it was more this month than last.

I asked Gray Suit if there was any way he could consolidate our statements and present them on a single page. Absolutely, he assured me. I'll get right on it. Each month I would tear open the envelope from the brokerage firm and find the same thick packet of unintelligible information. Finally I worked up the nerve to suggest that perhaps things weren't "working out." Gray Suit leaped up from his desk and extended his hand, relieved to see us go.

A friend had recommended a pair of brokers at another firm who had "done well" for him, as he put it. One had a full head of gorgeously coiffed hair; the other was bald. They were an odd couple, the Mutt and Jeff of Morgan Stanley. Mutt was young, maybe thirty, a junior partner hungry to rise through the ranks. Jeff was nearing retirement. They had a plan—not throwing darts at the board. Mutt and Jeff believed in building a portfolio composed only of stocks that met a long list of specific criteria: the company had to be of a certain size; its top managers had to have been in place for a stipulated period of time; its stock price had to be within a certain range . . . and so on. By never deviating from these rules, they could ensure that their investment choices were virtually risk-free. They had made a chart on a giant pasteboard poster. On our first visit, they leaned the chart on a chair and talked us through their theory. It made sense to me.

The Plan—as I came to think of it—had clearly worked for them. Kindly, soft-spoken, bespectacled Jeff had made a lot of money in his decades on the Street; he and his wife, an artist whose bold abstract works hung in his firm's waiting room, had a house in East Hampton and a cavernous apartment on Fifth Avenue filled with avant-garde art. They were major collectors. We were invited over to view their art—a Damien Hirst basketball floating in a fishtank, a Joseph Beuys furry spoon, a Schnabel cracked-plate collage. High-end art. Mutt, too, had artistic inclinations to go with his new wealth, as evinced by his Greenwich address. He was a modern dance buff, inviting us to the New York City Ballet and Alvin Ailey at BAM. He was also something of a gourmand and shared with us his favorite restaurants; "It's Umbrian, very special," he assured us of "an adorable little place in the neighborhood" that to my untutored palate seemed merely Italian.

A year after we signed on with Mutt and Jeff, the CEO of one of our trio of holdings dropped dead of a heart attack; the company's stock price dropped by 40 percent. Within a month Mutt had left the firm "to pursue other opportunities" and Jeff had decided to retire.

Weary pilgrims on the brokerage trail, we once again arranged for the transfer of our assets, applying to brokers Dr. Johnson's famous adage about second marriages: the triumph of hope over experience. Our goal—our investment strategy, if you will—had been considerably scaled down by now: instead of hoping to see our savings "amortize" over a lifetime, leaving us at the age of sixty-five a pair of white-haired and pink-cheeked retirees wealthy enough to buy a two-bedroom condo in Naples, Florida, we were happy when we didn't lose money.

This time we pinned our hopes on Open Shirt, who worked out of his apartment on the Upper East Side, answering his own phone and doing transactions at a Charles Schwab office around the corner. (A bad sign?) Open Shirt couldn't have been nicer. He, too, sweated tirelessly on our behalf, meeting with us each month in the alarmingly spare living room of his apartment to go over our investments. Open Shirt was clearly proud of his homework: on a glass coffee table he spread out neat bar graphs and pie charts, the better to size up our losses at a glance.

Open Shirt lasted less than a year, during which interval he managed to lose twenty thousand dollars in a bull market. When we announced that we were moving on, he was devastated. "Was there something I didn't do?" Besides making money, or at least staying even, you mean? These breakups were tough on all parties. Who would have thought that finding a good money manager was almost as hard as finding a spouse?

There were others: a tough-minded woman who had shattered the glass ceiling on Wall Street but couldn't decipher her own data; a mole-like mathematics Ph.D. who spun out abstruse discourses on probability theory and the bell curve. One broker liked to track his results by means of 3-D blocks that resembled high-rises—descending, steplike, month by month. A mere twenty or thirty phone calls and notarized letters later, we'd have a new broker frowning over our portfolio and promising the moon. ("By the time you retire you'll be worth ten times what you're worth now.")

How did they do it? These brokers couldn't have amassed enough money for Peter Duchin bands and houses in Greenwich and weird-looking high-price-tag works of art on the same 1.2 percent we were making. Did they have some private, income-yielding fund that was closed to us? Was there a secret society you had to belong to in order to get a better yield? Some kind of Masonic handshake that got you in the door? I brooded endlessly over this mystery. The lyrics of a Bob Dylan song ran through my head: *Something is happening, but you don't know what it is, do you, Mr. Jones?*

In the summer of 1979, not long after we moved to New York, we went in on a house-share in Southampton with a friend. It wasn't that expensive—I forget how much, but manageable on our modest young-people salaries—and we thought it would be nice to get out of town on hot summer weekends when the city was empty. Where was everyone? It turned out that anyone who could afford to left town—and by "anyone" I mean from kids just out of college who got time-shares in houses with twenty other kids to moguls who flew out to the eastern tip of Long Island on Friday afternoons in their private helicopters.

George, my friend who had arranged the rental, assured us that it was a comfortable turn-of-the-century house, with three bedrooms and a nice yard; but he warned me that it was "north of the highway"— whatever that meant. He wasn't going to be there the first weekend of our rental—Memorial Day weekend—and Anna was working, so I went out by myself. I took a late train that got in around midnight. When I got off at the Southampton station, there was a single broken-down taxi in the parking lot. I gave the driver our address, and he drove off, winding through streets darkened by bowers of leafy trees that shone like a Magritte in the hazy glow of streetlamps. He let me off in front of a modest two-story shingled house with a front porch. I groped for the key, let myself in, made a brief inspection of the premises—a living room with oval rugs, a rocker, and a plump couch; cozy bedrooms with Victorian wallpaper; a kitchen with an old white-enameled stove—and went to bed. I had no idea where I was.

The next morning I got up and went for a run. I wasn't certain which way the ocean was, but I could sense its general direction from the pale washed-out sky that indicates water. I crossed a busy two-lane road—was this the highway that my friend had referred to when he described to me where the house was? If so, then I was headed in the right direction—south, toward the ocean.

The road was wide and empty, lined on both sides by ancient elms with gnarled, root-braided trunks. Behind them, set farther back from the curb, were high, perfectly trimmed hedges. As I ran along, I glanced through a gap. There, at the end of a long graveled driveway, was something I had never seen before: a gray-shingled mansion, three stories high, its roof adorned with a thicket of chimneys. The front door had a fanlight over it. A white-pillared porch surrounded the house. The lawn was an emerald green expanse that shone in the sunlight. I stood at the entrance and stared. What could this be? The sight was impossible to take in at first: the house rose like an apparition in the distance, as remote and unreachable as the Castle in Kafka's novel that K longingly beholds. I was disoriented. Did people really live this way?

My mind groped for an analog, some work of literature that could help explain what I was looking at. It came to me unbidden and obvious: the Long Island home of Tom and Daisy in *The Great Gatsby*, whose lawn "started at the beach and ran toward the front door for a quarter of a mile, jumping over sun-dials and brick walls and burning gardens—finally when it reached the house drifting up the side in bright vines as though from the momentum of its run."

I stood gazing at the house for a long time and then resumed my run toward the sea. As I ran, I passed other gaps in the hedge and other houses as large as the one before which I had loitered like a pilgrim who arrives, after an arduous journey on dusty roads from some provincial town, at the massive and stupefying edifice of a cathedral infinitely larger than any structure he could ever have imagined on this earth. Baffled by the wealth beyond reckoning that must have been required to build such a dwelling, I recalled Keats's poem "On First Looking into Chapman's *Homer*," in which he imagines himself "like some watcher of the skies / When a new planet swims into his ken." Southampton was Oz-like, a mirage. Who lived in those houses behind the hedges? Bankers, businessmen, Old Money? I didn't have a clue.

Early on a Sunday morning in 2003, I'm at the breakfast table in our New York apartment when I hear the familiar thump of the Sunday *New York Times* on our doorstep. I lug the paper back to the table, preparing for the long slog—Styles, The City, The Week in Review— and a glossy brochure slips out. It's a real estate insert from the Corcoran Group. I sit beneath our shelf of dusty window plants and pore over the bewildering array of Fifth Avenue "maisonettes," Hamptons houses, and Bedford horse farms depicted on page after page of the fat brochure. So many! By now I've been in New York a quarter of a century. I have grown accustomed to reading about the very rich in the society pages of the *Times*, in *Architectural Digest* and *Vanity Fair*. I have peered through the windows of town houses on the Upper East Side and glimpsed drawing rooms with chandeliers; I have on rare occasions been in such homes myself, or in Park Avenue apartments where the eye must accustom itself to artworks normally seen in the great museums of the world. I have traveled abroad and know by now that Southampton, which on first encounter struck me as like no other place on earth, is replicated in every city, state, and nation—English country houses, Italian villas, French châteaux. The mega-rich are not a mere handful of the insanely fortunate; the annual list of the Forbes 400 doesn't mean that there are four hundred vastly wealthy people in the world. Those are the four hundred richest of what, it now appears, is an actual percentage of the human population.

Even so, the Corcoran Group catalog bewilders me. Who has $27 million to spend on a forty-room house in Beverly Hills? I try to calculate: say you have two hundred houses displayed in the catalog. Does that mean there are twenty thousand such houses in existence? Or more? On this subject, I'm as ignorant as I was twenty-five years ago. I now know that wealth on this scale exists; I have empirical evidence. What I don't know is how many people possess it.

Somehow, though, it feels as if there are more than there used to be. That there is more *talk* about these people I'm certain. Chroniclers of the dot-com boom marvel at the fortunes amassed by twenty-seven-year-old Internet geniuses and the venture capitalists who fund them. At the end of the year, a *Wall Street Journal* headline trumpets that $10 billion has been handed out in bonuses. I gaze slack-jawed in front of the TV set as Robin Leach takes us into the privates lives of *The Lifestyles of the Rich and Famous.* For the junior set, there is *MTV Cribs,* which takes my son, Will, into the homes of rap stars. In the *Times*'s Sunday Business section, the salaries of CEOs are microscopically scrutinized by "compensation experts" who have instant access to every corner-office pay stub in the land.

Nor is it just the seven-, eight-, and nine-figure guys whose bank accounts are public knowledge. Even in my lower-upper-middle-class media world, people seem to know to the nickel everyone else's salary, or "package." Word gets around. "He's gotta be pulling down a quarter of a million," a colleague announces with complete assurance when someone in our office gets a big promotion. (Is that *with* benefits?) A writer I know publishes a best seller and moves to a big house on the North Shore of Long Island. He's rumored to have been seen at a boutique art gallery on Madison Avenue that specializes in nineteenth- and twentieth-century European prints. "All of a sudden he's a collector," reports a friend who's been to the house. He spotted a signed Matisse in the front hall. I sit down for lunch at a fashionable restaurant with a friend who has gotten a great job as a columnist for a major newsweekly. He's also got a book contract and a movie deal. The maître d' knows him and comes over to shake hands. Men with recognizable faces—TV commentators, owners of newspapers and magazines, real estate tycoons—occupy the other tables. The cutlery gleams on the blindingly white tablecloth. "I'm making a shitload of money," my friend announces—and then names the exact sum. Panic clutches my chest. What did I do wrong? A line from Roethke pops into my head: "I run, I run to the whistle of money."

I dance to this tune as readily as anyone. I'm like Mrs. Kish, the mother in Delmore Schwartz's story "America! America!" When her son Edmund is visited at home by a friend renowned for his erudition, Edmund says to his mother, "You have just seen a genius"—to which Mrs. Kish replies, "How much money does he make?" Mrs. Kish, your question is one we'd all like to ask, but don't. A journalist whose byline I often see in *The New York Review of Books*—and who, I happen to know, lives in a town house on the Upper East Side and summers in Rhinebeck—invites me to lunch at that old WASP fortress the Racquet

& Tennis Club, on Park Avenue. The place is like a Peter Arno cartoon (excuse me, *drawing*): pale, ancient waiters shuffle among linen-covered tables beneath sparkling chandeliers. My host informs me, awkwardly, that he has "independent means." That's an interesting phrase: What does it mean? Does he have four million dollars? Ten million dollars? A hundred million dollars? I haven't a clue. Numbers on that scale mean about as much to me as the nonsense number a friend's child used to shout when she was four: "Eleventy-twenty." That's it: he has eleventy-twenty million dollars.

The provenance of Old Money I can understand in a vague sort of way from the American history courses I took in college: they got here first, claimed land, built railroads, founded banks. But what do the people who live in the huge mansions rising up in Westwood and the Hamptons and the northern suburbs of Chicago do for a living? As far as I can tell, many of them own companies that make stuff, though I'm not sure what: car parts, office furniture, wire hangers, transistor chips, "valves." Or they're "developers"—they build high-rises, shopping centers, malls.

At least these are things I can see: they're tangible. What really perplexes me is the question of what people "in financial services" do. For instance, investment bankers. What do they invest in? How does it work? I study a photograph in the Business section of the *Times* that shows a table of broad-shouldered men ordering magnums of Château Margaux at two thousand dollars a bottle in a private room at the 21 Club after closing a deal. What kind of deal? One night over rolled stuffed grape leaves in a local Turkish restaurant, my friend Michael, a banker at a venerable Wall Street brokerage house, tried to explain his arcane trade. "It's all about relationships. Say I know about a company that's looking for capital. It's a growing firm. There's a good bet that it's going to make it—but it needs money now. There's another company,

venture capitalists looking to invest. Their job is to find promising companies, pour money into them, and take a percentage—a big percentage—of the profits. So you say, 'Why don't I put you guys together' and
I'll get a chunk of dough as my fee for brokering the deal—and maybe
even a percentage of the deal."

One of the reasons why I have trouble grasping the mechanics of
these transactions is that they bore me. I'm not interested. As the child
of liberal Jewish parents, I inherited their conviction that money didn't
matter. My father, especially, endorsed this attitude; he used to chortle
and exclaim over the iconoclastic editorials in the *Carolina Israelite*. A
great reader, he celebrated the works of the Modernists not only for
their literary breakthroughs—their radical exploration of consciousness and their willingness to challenge the authority of conventional
narrative—but also for their indifference to wealth and power. The
money troubles of James Joyce and the way he'd been spurned by his
homeland held great appeal for my father; he repeated to me stories
gleaned from Richard Ellmann's biography: Joyce borrowed money
from his friends to leave Ireland; he had to work as a translator for
Berlitz in Trieste; he badgered his patron, Sylvia Beach, to set up a fund
for his support. The artist, by the very terms of his vocation, had sen-
tenced himself to a vow of poverty. Antimaterialism went hand in hand
with genius.

Anyway, this was the myth. My father's protestation of indifference
masked a deep ambivalence about money. "While everyone else was getting rich, I was in the laundry room making oboe reeds out of bamboo
and fish skin," he told me ruefully one day. On the surface, it didn't
matter. My parents had what they needed for a comfortable life: the
house in the suburbs, the two cars, the trips to Europe. They didn't have
a lot, but they didn't seem to need a lot. I don't recall them ever dis-
cussing money around the dinner table. On my father's salary—I

remember the number: $36,000—you could buy the goods that ordinary Americans of our class could reasonably expect to possess. There was a shiny grille on the patio, an abundance of lawn furniture, a power mower in the garage. The hall closet was crammed with tennis rackets.

The problem was that many of his friends had more. Not all—there was the shoe salesman, Gene, a violinist in my father's chamber-music group who longed to be a professional violinist; and Leonard, who lost his restaurant and ended his life as the kitchen supervisor at an old people's home. But many of them prospered—they had resourcefulness and energy and lived through a time of prosperity not unlike the time we live in now. They built companies: they made gaskets, textiles, shirts. They bought second homes in Miami and Palm Springs. They weren't ostentatious, but it was a tight-knit community; everyone knew what everyone else had. And if you didn't have, you felt it, no matter what you said.

I've inherited this ambivalence—the nagging sense that one *ought* to have money. Only it's exacerbated by the boom of the 1990s. And not just in money-marinated New York. Out in La Jolla, where my parents lived before they moved east, it seemed as if Qualcomm had made the whole community rich. Its founder was a local pioneer in cell phone technology, Irwin Jacobs, and word about the company spread around town well before Wall Street got wind of it. "My grandma made a killing," crowed my niece. My mother, disregarding a tip from her hairdresser, Teddy—the wife of the company's founder was a client, which is how he knew when the Japanese cell phone market was poised for takeoff—missed out, as usual. "Why didn't you tell me?" I upbraided her. "I don't know, dear. It never would have occurred to me."

Another lost opportunity. "You feel foolish if you're not rich," a famous New York intellectual confessed to me at a moment when financial commentators were predicting the Dow would eventually hit

30,000. Maureen Dowd, in a column just after the AOL/Time Warner merger, complained that she felt "guilty" about not being a millionaire. "I never cared about money before," she wrote in bafflement: "It was not what Country Joe and the Fish taught me to value." The novelist Colin Harrison expressed anxiety about missing the boat in a *Times* op-ed piece, scribbling down conversations overheard in a Starbucks near Silicon Alley, home of the New York–based dot-com start-ups clustered around the Flatiron Building: "There ought to be a valuation of $60 million . . ." "He started with a hundred million dollars . . ." Even the *New York Post*'s Andrea Peyser, a woman with a seemingly bottomless reserve of disdain, seemed rattled by the boom. "You were sick of feeling like an outsider at the banquet, nose pressed against the glass separating you from gluttony," she confessed. "Yet inside, you feared it was some weakness on your own part, some lack of smarts or creativity or courage, that prevented you from taking your seat at the table."

Why is it that what others have makes us question what we have? What difference does it make if my friend who made shrewd investments owns a BMW and I don't? Let's say I inhabited a world in which BMWs didn't exist: no one had one. Everyone drove Subarus. The anxiety, the humiliation induced by the fact that I can't afford a BMW and my friend can—that anxiety would be gone. I turn on *Charlie Rose* and there is a guy I know who has just published a book, talking animatedly at the round table. Instantly my stomach knots up: his book will sell, he'll make money, he'll buy a BMW. Already he emanates a prosperous air. Once a scruffy intellectual whose jackets looked as if they were off the rack at the Salvation Army Store, he's wearing a tailor-made herringbone suit; his beard is trim, and he's clearly gotten his hair cut at some exclusive men's salon where they glaze it and put you under a dryer. My life is exactly the same as it was before I turned on the TV;

nothing has changed. Yet I'm tormented. Watching my friend babble on about his book has forced me to take a detailed inventory of my entire life: what I own, what I've achieved, above all who I am. How else can you measure yourself except by comparison?

One of my favorite books is Leonard Woolf's five-volume memoir of his life and times. Leonard was the husband of Virginia Woolf and known in his day as an influential journalist and as the cofounder, with John Lehmann, of the Hogarth Press. The Woolfs never had much money: Virginia Woolf famously enumerated a writer's needs as five hundred pounds per annum and a room of one's own, and that was about what they had. (Five hundred pounds was a lot more in 1915 than it is today, but it wasn't a lot even then.) They "divided their time"—as people say nowadays who are trying to indicate without bragging that they have two houses—between their town house in Tavistock Square and their Sussex country place, Monks House, which didn't even have running water until the success of one of Virginia's books enabled them to install a bathroom—they called it "Mrs. Dalloway's lavoratory." For many years they had no car; they alighted from the train in a nearby town and walked through the country lanes to their house in the dark. Virginia supplemented their meager income from a trust that provided dividends amounting to four hundred pounds a year, from modest advances on her novels, and from the articles she churned out for the *Times Literary Supplement.* Leonard, a self-described "introspective intellectual," hacked away as a political journalist and as the literary editor of various publications. Virginia Woolf identified him to her friend and lover Vita Sackville-West as "a penniless Jew."

Leonard Woolf's memoir is notable for its candor, and one of the subjects he doesn't shy away from is money. "Professional writers rarely reveal, even in autobiographies, accurately and in detail what exactly they earned by their books," he writes in volume 3, *Beginning Again.*

Woolf was determined to rectify this omission. "We started the Hogarth Press in 1917 on a capital of £41.15s.3d," he recalls, putting in tidy columns the exact profit and loss of each book he published. They needed £477 a year to live on; Virginia earned £100 from each of her first two novels; and so on: Journalism, Books, Total.

The success of *The Years*, a best seller in America, worked a profound change on their lives, but that wasn't until 1939, by which time they were both in their late fifties:

> *Neither of us was extravagant or had any desire for conspicuous extravagance; we did not alter fundamentally our way of life, because on £1,000 a year we already lived the kind of life we wished to live, and we were not going to alter the chosen pattern of our life because we made £6,000 in the year instead of £1,000. Within the material framework which we had chosen for our existence we got more of the things which we liked to possess—books, pictures, a garden, a car—and we did more of the things we wanted to do, for instance travel, and less in the occupations we did not want to do, for instance journalism.*

We did more of the things we wanted to do. I like the sound of that.

In the 1990s, I knew people—people like me, writers and editors and professors—who couldn't take the disparity between their admittedly comfortable lives and the lives of the millionaires they saw around them. Swept up in the tide of consumerism, they longed to possess what the rich possessed. "It's hard to go back to the library after you've spent your lunch hour in Hamburger Heaven reading that *Vanity Fair* piece about Palm Beach," an English professor friend of mine complains to me. I studied it myself. The homes in the photographs are stupendous, on a scale beyond the capacity of the human mind to grasp. The formal gardens, the clipped lawns, the pillared terraces seem literally out of this world. La Follia, the $50 million mansion built by the heiress Terry Allen Kramer, has a living room with a coffered ceiling, eighteenth-century furniture, and arched windows facing the ocean that descend into the floor at the flick of a switch. "One house is more beautiful than the other," says the heiress of a railroad fortune. "It's an enchanted world, a microcosm of highly civilized people who are only interested in being surrounded by beautiful objects and a beautiful environment."

Like the urchins in *Bleak House*—urchins with robust 401(k)s—the new entrepreneurs, refugees from academia and the arts, have dreamed up ways to join the ranks of the rich. A friend started an Internet company designed to provide news digests to people too harried to keep themselves informed. Another started a magazine for the dot-com industry. Still others have taken more conventional routes, enrolling in business school at forty. A neighbor of mine, a high school English teacher who couldn't stand earning $60,000 a year, got an MBA from the Wharton School and joined a Wall Street firm. Does he miss teaching Yeats to sixteen-year-olds, the familiar lines kindling a surge of joy each year as he cracks open his worn anthology of *Twentieth-Century English Verse*? *I will talk no more of books or the long war* . . . I have to admit that he seems happy as he loads up his BMW parked in front of the building on a Friday afternoon, the back filled to the brim with golf clubs and tennis rackets, the kids, two lanky good-humored boys, fighting over who gets to sit where as they head up to the Berkshires. Besides, he still reads Yeats; he hasn't lost his soul.

I also have friends who've taken a different route—they've chosen the 1960s over the 1990s. One of my friends, a physician, talks of joining Doctors Without Borders in a few years and going off to Africa. Another, who's made a pot of money on Wall Street, teaches math in an inner-city public school. Social philanthropy—a new concept that arose out of the vast "wealth-creation" of the last decade—is on the rise. People who cashed out their stock options at Microsoft or Intel are tutoring kids in the inner cities, running for city council, organizing the homeless. "I have all the things in life I need," says a lawyer who has devoted her post–Silicon Valley life to defending murderers on death row. "A nice apartment in Park Slope, a car, a summer cottage in the Poconos: what else could I possibly want?"

Most of us, though, don't have the option—at least right now—of rekindling our old political passions. We sit hunched over the growing pile of bills in our drawer that urgently demand attention—the lawyer's charge for the refinancing of our co-op; the mortgage bill; the credit card bills for God knows what; and the most alarming bill of all, the kids' tuition. The kids: a seemingly depthless money pit. I glance up from scribbling a check to the *Times*'s Remember the Neediest campaign when the hovering presence of my tall son darkens my desk like a giant redwood casting its shadow on the forest floor. "Dad," he says sweetly, "you owe me forty dollars." Forty dollars! That used to be the kind of money I'd get for my birthday—if I pooled my parents' twenty and my grandmas' ten each. "Where'd you get that number?" "It's two weeks' allowance and you forgot to pay me last week. I have it in my computer." He invites me to his room and clicks on a neatly entered line of dates, with check marks beside those on which the money has been paid. I hand over two twenties. My son has just performed what a friend calls a "cashectomy."

The question for many of us now is: will we get to the finish line? Squeezed by globalization, even members of the privileged middle and upper middle class are beginning to feel the pain. Job security, the gold watch at retirement, is a thing of the past. I have friends who've been at the same company for their entire lives and are now being pressured to accept buyouts, saving the company the generous salaries that go with two or three decades of loyalty and enabling it to hire younger people at reduced rates. I have friends who've been "terminated," the victims of "workforce reduction," given a half hour to clean out their desks before being escorted from the building by security guards. One of my friends, who got fired from a brokerage firm two years ago, still hasn't found another job; he belongs to a support group for the unemployed.

Over lunch one day, a veteran journalist I know who has struggled to put it together over several hard-contested decades pushes aside his untouched salade niçoise, fires up a Marlboro Light, and sighs: "Well, I've just paid the last tuition bill for my third kid. I can die now."

The dwindling family coffers, eroded by losses sustained in the stock market plunge, offer little prospect of relief. My mother talks hopefully about the modest inheritance my brother, Steve, and I will receive, but she's not going anywhere soon. Insanely compulsive health-consciousness—the spooning out of cottage cheese, counting the grapes on the plate—and advances in medical technology have combined to produce a new demographic: the Old Old. By 2050, I read somewhere, more than 5 percent of the population will be over eighty-five—the fastest-growing age group in America. "I saw the Flakowitzes," my mother reports, back from a trip to Chicago. They were our next-door neighbors when I was growing up on the North Shore: Dr. Flakowitz was a dentist. I remember his wife, Miriam, in their garden, a babushka around her head, on her hands and knees planting tulip bulbs. "He's ninety-four and she's ninety-one. Can you believe it?" A childhood friend I run into at a party informs me that her father has just celebrated his hundredth birthday. Soon they'll achieve biblical longevity: I can imagine my mother saying, "I just saw Mrs. Stolberg at the grocery store. She's a hundred and eighty. Can you believe it?"

I'm not a ghoul. I like having Mom around. Sunday lunch at Brookhaven is a festive occasion; the ladies in their trim jackets and cashmere sweaters are saucy and youthful, the tiny tribe of still-living widowers elegant in their parrot-hued country club jackets. It's Mom who harps on this theme. "I can't afford to go to La Jolla this winter. I'm invading capital."

"That's why it's there," I retort. "What are you saving for? Retirement?"

"I'm saving it for you."

"For God's sake, spend it. Go. I have enough."

How much is enough? If you have, say, a nice apartment or house, a few hundred thousand socked away in a 401(k), and another hundred thousand or two in equities, you are rich by any standard save the unattainable strata of Palm Beach denizens or the inhabitants of that imposing canyon of vast apartments piled atop one another on Park Avenue like the cave dwellings of the Santa Clara Pueblo. Would it be fun to have more? Yes. It would be fun to sit at the table of Smith & Wollensky with a marbled slab of one-hundred-dollar Kobe beef on my plate, my pink-and-blue-patterned tie from Turnbull & Asser loosened around the collar of my shirt. What else? Let's see: a high-ceilinged apartment on Central Park West with a stunning view of the reservoir; a big, gray-shingled house on the Vineyard; a Lexus or an Audi. (I used to covet a Range Rover, but that was in another time—before I turned fifty, before my father died, before the planes went into the World Trade Center. A Range Rover would be an embarrassment now, linked to drilling for oil in Alaska, global warming, and the destruction of caribou habitats.) "Money is a mood enhancer," says my friend Edgar, who cashed in stock options on an Internet start-up and bought a house in Connecticut with the proceeds. It's true: putting on a crisp new shirt from Brooks Brothers (it doesn't have to be from Turnbull & Asser) makes me feel prosperous; it reminds me of that Dylan Thomas line, "my red veins full of money." But it doesn't provide the adrenaline rush it once did.

I have a new idea about what financial success would mean to me. Not the country house refurbished with antiques; not the vacations at Canyon Ranch or the Golden Door; not a fancy car. Of course, I do want these things. When I gaze at the TV advertisement for a Jaguar, hugging the windy road that runs beside the Pacific Ocean, its wheels glinting in the California sun, I don't think: Nah. Who needs it? My heart aches—fleetingly—to own the Jaguar. But my heart also aches to be free of the desire to own it. "I want, I want, I want," says Henderson the Rain King, the eponymous hero of Saul Bellow's novel. I want not to want.

Failure

The year I turned fifty I was fired from a job. I hadn't been doing well in the job. I didn't have my heart in it, and it showed. I wasn't making a significant contribution. I was superfluous. It was just a matter of time.

Anxious about my performance, I had already gone to see my boss once. "I don't feel encouraged," I had said to him. "I'm not invited to meetings, I'm not given assignments." He was new to the job; I had flourished under the previous boss, who had hired me and given me a lot of responsibility.

My new boss had been gracious but perfunctory. "You work here, you belong here. There's all kinds of stuff for you to do, but you're the one who has to make it work." He called out to his secretary. He was awaiting a report and wanted to know if it had arrived. "Stop worrying," he said, and rose from his chair to see me out.

Three months later, I got a call from his secretary asking if I could come in to see him the following week: Thursday at three o'clock.

Why had he summoned me? It was a call I'd been waiting for without out quite knowing it. But when his secretary called, my stomach knotted up; my mind became strangely blank.

The days passed slowly. I could think of nothing else. Endless scenarios played themselves out in my head as I went about my work. He was going to propose that I take on a special assignment. He was going to ask for advice on some matter. But I knew what it was about. You always know.

I got to his office at ten of three and sat down in the waiting room. I picked up a three-week-old issue of *Newsweek* and leafed through it uncomprehendingly—something about the dangers of high cholesterol. I glanced at my watch every minute—sometimes twice a minute. The secretary sat at her desk talking on the phone in a low voice, her hand cupped over her mouth so that I couldn't hear. Was she talking about me? She was young, in her early twenties, and had on a short black dress and a tight sleeveless white blouse. At two minutes after three her intercom buzzed. She put the other call on hold, listened briefly, and told me I could go in.

It was a nice corner office, with slatted wood blinds over the windows, mahogany bookshelves, a table piled high with magazines. The furniture was sleek but comfortable—white fabric everywhere—and the room had a casual, unpretentious air about it, more like a college dorm than a chief executive's office. The books on the shelves weren't for show; they were the books of a person who read books. The covers were scuffed, the lettering faded. The newspapers scattered about on couches and tables and chairs looked as if they'd been gone through that morning. Clearly, work—intellectual work—got done here.

My boss came out from around his desk and shook my hand. He motioned me toward a chair and sat down on a couch across from me. He had on khakis and a striped blue-and-white shirt open at the neck. I'd hardly ever seen him in a tie; he was confident, at ease with himself. This wasn't a corporation and he wasn't an executive, his dress-down style was meant to communicate. It was a place where creative, interesting people worked. Hierarchies didn't matter. He'd never been a manager himself until he was tapped for the job; he'd been one of us, and the open-necked shirt made the statement that he was still one of us.

He was a handsome man, tall, vigorous, with tousled black hair. He was a full decade younger than me. (Nearly everyone I worked for was younger than me these days.) He hadn't sought the job; it had probably never occurred to him that he would one day be running the company in which he'd distinguished himself on the other side of the desk. But he had been a star there, and it was a self-enclosed, intimate fiefdom. It was natural for management to be reluctant to "go outside" when the time came to recruit a new leader. Now he was management himself. He didn't sit around like the rest of us, waiting for the boss's attention: he *was* the boss.

He seemed uneasy. "I don't want to drag this out," he said. "I'm not going to renew your contract." We didn't have actual "jobs"—we had renewable contracts, usually by the year, and no benefits. But the fact remained: however you put it, I was being fired.

He looked at me. I looked at him. "I can't afford it," he went on, brusque and efficient—or, at any rate, trying to be brusque and efficient. This was all new territory. "I need to bring in people who can do the work." He reached down and grabbed a can of Diet Coke off the table.

What was I supposed to say? What was the protocol for getting fired? Did you leap up and storm out of the room? Burst into tears? Be mature and help him out? *I quite understand. I'm sure this must be tough for you. Don't give it another thought.* In some region of my mind, I thought he was just floating an idea; it was hypothetical. I was welcome to stay on if I wanted.

Something was happening to me that had happened to so many people before me. I was undergoing a nearly archetypal experience—

like watching a child being born or losing a parent. This was one of the events that life threw your way. My chest tightened; I could hardly breathe. In front of me on the desk was a small round bronze clock. It said five after three. Was it possible that I had only been here for three minutes? It felt as though I'd been sitting in this chair for hours. I noticed that the cuff of my shirt was frayed.

The room had the eerie silence that comes over the landscape just before a storm, when the dark clouds are gathering in the distance. Birds cease their cheeping and everything is still. I could hear the bleat of traffic down below on Forty-second Street, trucks grinding their gears at a light. I felt alert, aware of the panic clawing at my throat.

It was time to get up and leave, but I wasn't ready. I thought of Willy Loman refusing to leave his boss's office the day he's fired. *You'll have to excuse me, Willy, I gotta see some people. Pull yourself together.*

"Why can't you just put me on a reduced contract?" I pleaded.

"Because I can't afford it. I'm on a tight budget." His predecessor had spent a fortune throwing lavish parties, hiring expensive consultants, handing out lucrative contracts. Our expense accounts had been limitless. It was a different company now. The new chief executive had been instructed by the company's owner to enforce a measure of fiscal discipline.

"But what am I going to do? I've got a family to support."

"That's why I asked you in now," he said. His face softened. This was no fun for him either. "Your contract isn't up for three months. That should give you time to find something."

He stood up. The interview was over.

That night, I took Will to a Rangers game. It was near the end of the season, and Madison Square Garden was two-thirds empty. The seats we had ended up with were the two worst in the house—the last row in the last tier. Will looked miserable. I couldn't stand the idea of having both of us be miserable, and the idea of feeling pinched and poor was intolerable on a day when I had just lost my job. We descended the escalators to the box office and bought front-row seats behind the Rangers' bench.

As I watched the players flying up and down the rink and downed my third Dewar's in a plastic cup, queasy about what the three-hundred-dollar charge for our two tickets would do to my next month's Visa bill, I tried to get my head around the fact that I had now been in New York for twenty years. What a bumpy ride: Were all lives like this? Was it a condition of existence that it never reached a plateau of even momentary equilibrium? I had come here at the age of twenty-eight, the provincial staking out his literary claim. I had been intoxicated by the city, a kingdom of limitless aspiration, of vast and uncharted possibility. The writer's pilgrimage from the provinces to the capital was a story as familiar to me as a Grimm fairy tale. Like the London to which Dr. Johnson made his determined way from the rural village of Litchfield, New York was the logical—the only—destination for a young man in postwar America who harbored ambitions to write. New York was where people went who wanted to make something of themselves. How I knew this at such an early age isn't clear to me even now, but the major events and decisions in my life—what career to choose, where to live, even how to feel—were gotten from books.

My head was filled with images of Edmund Wilson, our preeminent man of letters, settling down in Greenwich Village in the 1920s and embarking on his ambitious literary career. I read with high excitement Wilson's journals, *The Twenties,* which chronicled the decade when he was writing for *Vanity Fair,* lunching at the Coffee House with the magazine's editor, Frank Crowninshield, beavering away at his desk on West Twelfth Street through "the heaviness and undress of summer"—what a marvelously sensuous phrase that was! I had filed away F. Scott Fitzgerald's evocation, in *The Crack-Up,* of venturing out into the city "through strange doors into strange apartments with intermittent swings along in taxis through the soft nights." I was gripped by the story of Dreiser's *Sister Carrie* arriving in New York amid the "darkness and smoke" of the tunnel beneath Park Avenue and hearing the conductor cry "Grand Central Station!" I read Alfred Kazin's lyrical memoir of growing up in Brooklyn, *A Walker in the City,* over and over, thrilled by his description of the armored knights in the Metropolitan Museum, the gray whale "floating dreamlike on wires from the ceiling" in the Museum of Natural History, the skaters in Central Park: it was all there, waiting for me.

Rangers stomped in and out of the box, throwing open the low door and charging out onto the ice. I was always comparing my life to the lives of others and found myself thinking of Isaac Rosenfeld, a classmate of Saul Bellow's at Tuley High School in the 1930s. Rosenfeld, like his best friend Bellow, was a book-besotted Chicago boy with limitless ambition; Tuley classmates thought Isaac was the one who would go the distance. He and Bellow attended the University of Chicago together and were in lockstep until Rosenfeld beat him to New York, the city that, then as now, represented the apotheosis of all cultural ambition. While Bellow was still brooding on park benches in Chicago, Rosenfeld was rapidly making a name for himself as a critic. But he ran into heavy mental weather, became a Reichian, got divorced, suffered crippling writer's block, and came to a poignant end. "He died in a seedy, furnished room on Walton Street, alone," wrote Bellow in a preface to Rosenfeld's posthumous collection of essays: "a bitter death to his children, his wife, his lovers, his father."

This story fascinated me. What would have happened if Rosenfeld had lived? Would the furnished room on Walton Street have come to be seen as the place where he'd weathered a crisis? *That was a tough time when I was living on Walton Street; I thought I'd never get through it.* Or would it have been the beginning of the end, the moment when his life took a turn from which he would never recover? Who could say? He brought to mind Housman's poem "To an Athlete Dying Young."

> *Smart lad, to slip betimes away*
> *From fields where glory does not stay,*
> *And early though the laurel grows*
> *It withers quicker than the rose.*

Why smart? Because he had escaped before the inevitable erosion of his early promise.

He hadn't had time to fail.

The idea that failure may be cathartic is alien to our culture. We have no patience for imperfection, no belief in the pedagogic value of the flaw, the lapse, the error in judgment. Yet failing is the foundation upon which genuine achievement is built. It gives us the tools—humility, self-knowledge, desperation—to persist. "It's not enough to fail," writes the poet and critic James Fenton: "You have to come to feel your failure, to live it through, to turn it over in your hand, like a stone with strange markings. You have to wake up in the middle of the night and hear it whistling around the roof, or chomping in the field below, like some loyal horse—my failure, my very own failure."

One night when they were maybe thirteen and nine I took my children to see *Mr. Holland's Opus*. This is the movie, if you recall, where Richard Dreyfuss plays a high school music teacher with a deaf child and major frustration over the fact that he didn't end up a famous composer and had to settle for conducting an orchestra of pimply kids. I wept through the whole movie. Dreyfuss having a fight with his impaired kid and then tearfully making up; Dreyfuss yelling at the orchestra's hapless tympanist for losing the beat, then praising him tenderly when he gets it right; Dreyfuss being forced out of his job by a heartless principal: the paper napkin I'd gotten with my popcorn was twisted and soggy. Mr. Holland hadn't achieved all he might have wished to in life; he had, in his own eyes, failed. But he had also redeemed himself by giving something to the world. It was possible to survive the pain of falling short—and even to make something of it. At the end, when the stooped and white-haired music teacher, lured to the school auditorium on some pretext, walks in to find his former orchestra, now middle-aged themselves, on stage, instruments in hand, and the conductor brings down his baton with a swift and decisive chop and they begin to play the symphony on which Mr. Holland has been laboring for most of his life, it was too much; I broke down, my shuddering sobs causing people in the row in front of us to turn around and stare while my two mortified children gazed down at the grimy, popcorn-littered floor in mute alarm.

What's with Dad? they must have thought. How could they begin to grasp the power of my identification with this man? In their eyes, I was Dad, a man who went to work, came home with his bulging briefcase, and seemed to make his way in the world. He talked on the phone in a loud, authoritative voice. He was no hollow-cheeked loser, disheveled, wan, his tie askew. He provided for them, sat upright at the dinner table, helped them with homework. He had a closetful of suits. How could they intuit his conviction that he was a failure? There was no way to explain it—either to them or to himself. It existed within him, a condition that had no cause, no reason. It made no sense, yet he believed it to be true. *Don't you see, children? Your dad thinks he's Mr. Holland.*

It's a slow afternoon, and I'm scanning my shelves for something to read when I spy a thick maroon-bound volume: *The Class of 1971 Twenty-*

fifth Anniversary Report. At 1,305 pages, it's one of the longest books in my collection, right up there with my two-volume Proust—and one of the most haunting. What makes this anthology so compelling? I think it's the momentousness of the milestones being commemorated. We're not at the beginning, full of bravado and false hope; we're not at the end, glad that we haven't turned up in the obit column yet. We're just young enough to not quite believe in the prospect of our own imminent mortality yet mature enough to be taking stock. Also, let's admit it, there's a trace of there-but-for-the-grace-of-God involved, a fascination, however unseemly, with who made it and who didn't. As the notoriously unsentimental Gore Vidal put it, "It's not enough to succeed; one's friends must fail."

The candor of these discursive entries is jaw-dropping; everything is on the table, from nervous breakdowns to switches in sexual orientation, marital dysfunction to substance abuse. It's as if the audience, with its combination of intimacy—we're classmates, after all—and anonymity, has loosened up the contributors to blurt out the whole story. One classmate, whose brother and sister both died of cancer, writes, "Less painful, but more nagging, has been the recognition of the limits of my professional abilities." At forty-seven, he has discovered that he is "only one of many little guys in a field funded by a few giants," and he notes, "I don't think Stockholm will ever be calling." Another classmate, a former employee of the U.S. Postal Service, pours out an agonized lament over his inability to finish his dissertation, his failure to get married, to stay in a job: "If there's anything that sums up the past twenty-five years for me, it's a paucity of major commitments, i.e., to a specific career, to a woman. But my fundamental commitment deficit has been to myself, i.e., a reluctance to accept myself for what I am, both my strengths and my foibles." Don't any of these people have psychiatrists?

A few entries are tantalizingly grim. "The past five years have been the most harrowing and sobering of my life. All the comforts and material security I had come to expect, almost as a birthright, were taken away or squandered. In depression and rage, I toyed daily with self-destruction and depravity." Wow.

The successes, by contrast, emanate a cheery unreality. "I have been fortunate to live the American entrepreneurial dream," writes the founder of a multinational petroleum firm. "So far, the road has been smooth," writes a television executive in a sweetly self-effacing confession. A prominent newspaper columnist writes, "I ended up doing in life exactly what I fantasized about doing when I arrived—working for a newspaper and writing about politics," but goes on to acknowledge that the road has, in fact, not been quite smooth: "Still, that simple description of where I am now masks the turmoil, some of it painful, of the years between graduation and today: the agonizing collapse of a first marriage; the violent and premature death of my mother; the grotesquely premature death of friends."

And now the *Thirtieth* has just landed on my desk, mercifully thinner. Did people die? Some. ("On the same day, we each learned that we had cancer.") Many contributors to the *Twenty-fifth Reunion Book* have fallen silent, as if life itself, so bafflingly unknowable, has muted their will to make sense of it. Those who did weigh in sound cautiously hopeful, reconciled to the accumulating catastrophes of divorce, the deaths of parents, the dwindling of ambition. Acceptance is the dominant note. "Certainly there is much around my family life that is difficult, painful, and sad: alcoholism, divorce, death, and emotional distance. I see and feel these issues, but somehow I have found a balance between the highs and lows of my everyday life."

And these are the privileged ones, the high achievers. What about my friends from high school, many of them talented in one way or another, who faded out? What happened to Ben, who would down a six-pack of

Budweiser that he'd bought from a drunk in the parking lot of Howard Liquors, lock the door of his bedroom, turn a Roland Kirk album up full blast, and join in on his saxophone? I can see him now, eyes tightly shut, a Camel smoldering in the ashtray. He's vanished. Or the friend who wanted to be a documentary filmmaker and ended up writing ad copy, or the poet who studied Japanese and disappeared into a state mental institution. They, too, had promise, that radiant nimbus that surrounds the gifted— what a writer I know calls "the Shine." Unfortunately, they were also missing some other necessary quality: stamina, discipline, a tolerance for risk. Maybe they had intractable conflicts with their parents; maybe they were addiction-prone. Maybe they were poor and didn't have the luxury of failing and starting over. Maybe success just wasn't in the cards.

The American myth of self-creation has no room for variables over which we have no control: intelligence (successful people tend to have high IQs); temperament (energy, one of the primary indicators for success, is a biological trait); talent (a gifted pianist is born a pianist). Even emotional intelligence—a feel for how others feel—is innate. Yet we persist in seeing ourselves as masters of our destiny, architects of our own fate. The rich, the powerful, the well-known made it because they had the drive to make it. Period.

What of those for whom success goes uncelebrated? My friend who restores nineteenth-century photographs doesn't get his name on Page Six, but he's doing exactly what he wants to do. Does success have to be measured by celebrity or the recognition of one's peers? Can you declare yourself a success without the confirmation of others? That capacity, I've come to believe, is the key to happiness, or at least acceptance—which may be, when all is said and done, the definition of happiness. We inevitably fall short, no matter how successful we are in the eyes of the world; our ambition outstrips our capability. I myself must take the inventory of my achievements and determine how I've done. The examined life and the public life are by no means the same thing.

It's a school night in the winter of 1965, and I'm sitting in the basement of our house in Evanston, Illinois, transfixed by the black-and-white film on TV. Beside me on the couch are my father and mother. On the screen is Lee J. Cobb in the role of Willie Loman. The play is winding down as we sit there numb in a row, tears rolling down our cheeks. The last two hours have been wrenching, ghastly, like watching a car crash. At moments—the scene where Willy gets fired; the scene where Biff and Happy abandon Willy in the restaurant and go off with a pair of whores—I've been flooded with a desolation far beyond anything I could have imagined it was possible for a sixteen-year-old boy to feel. The house is still; a funereal silence settles over the room as Linda, Willy's wife, lays a wreath on his grave. I hear a car go by outside.

Then Charley, Willy's friend, is speaking:

Nobody dast blame this man. You don't understand: Willy was a salesman. And for a salesman, there is no rock bottom to the life. He don't put a bolt to a nut, he don't tell you the law or give you medicine. He's a man way out there in the blue, riding on a smile and a shoeshine. And when they start not smiling back—that's an earthquake. And then you get yourself a couple of spots on your hat, and you're finished. Nobody dast blame this man. A salesman is got to dream, boy. It comes with the territory.

What is my father thinking, sitting there with his hands on his knees? Is he thinking of his father, a timid man who came over on the boat from Russia with an engineering degree and mastery of half a dozen languages, only to end up running a corner drugstore on the Northwest

Side of Chicago? Or is he thinking of himself, not as timid as his father, but somehow not possessed of quite enough of that go-getter quality, prevented by his nature and his limitations from following his dream? What he had really wanted to be was a professional musician—to play the oboe in the Chicago Symphony Orchestra. But it was the Depression: he needed to make a living, and so he became a doctor—hardly a humiliating profession. After all, he didn't go into advertising (which isn't so humiliating either). His tragedy—or is that too strong a word?—was that he failed to achieve what he'd hoped to achieve. He wasn't a defeated man; he was a thwarted man: one of the most common human conditions.

"We're free," Linda is saying as Biff, Willy's other son, lifts her up and carries her off the stage. A flute plays softly as the lights go down. My mother and father and I are sobbing now, as devastated as if someone we love had died. I stumble upstairs to my room and sit at my desk, drained. I try to focus on my American history textbook—what was Manifest Destiny, anyway?—but I'm too haunted by Happy Loman's words to concentrate: *It's the only dream you can have—to come out number-one man.*

Many years later, I read Arthur Miller's memoir, *Timebends,* in which he gives an account of how he came to write this play. He had already experienced success with his first play, *All My Sons,* when he struck—or was struck by—his theme. As he wrote his play, hour after hour, day after day, he laughed and wept, stunned by the power of his discovery: that Willy Loman was a vessel designed to contain the essence of our human longing "to excel, to win out over anonymity and meaninglessness, to love and be loved, and above all, perhaps, to *count.*" That Miller expressed what so few writers ever manage to express, tapped something deep and powerful in the human psyche, was evident from the audience's response on opening night: "As sometimes happened later on during the run, there was no applause at the final curtain of the first performance. With the curtain down, some people stood to put their coats on and then sat again, some, especially men, were bent forward covering their faces, and others were openly weeping." I myself have had this experience, even with Willy Lomans—Dustin Hoffman and Brian Dennehy—who weren't quite up to the job. At the close of Dennehy's performance—a marathon of shouting, bellowing, and haranguing so strenuous that I worried at times he would collapse onstage—I was wrung out as I joined the tearful theatergoers filing ashen-faced from the Belasco Theatre like a procession of mourners. "Willy was representative everywhere, in every kind of system, of ourselves in this time," wrote Miller in his memoir—a daringly self-confident assessment, but true.

Yet I wonder if Miller's explanation for the play's success is right. He is at heart an optimist, blessed with the American belief that things work out in the end, and so perhaps oblivious to his own work's darker side. (Just because he wrote it doesn't mean he has to understand it.) But is it the play's let's-hear-it-for-the-little-guy message that makes people weep, or is it the experience of recognizing their own struggles with failure? The crushing reversals that Willy suffers—getting fired, being humiliated by his associates, watching his sons turn into losers—resonate because they're so familiar. "I don't know what to say," the director Elia Kazan stammers when Miller shows him a draft of his play. "My father . . ." "He broke off," Miller reports in his memoir, "the first of a great many men—and women—who would tell me that Willy was their father." Their father and, eventually, them. Like father, like son. The story of literature—and thus of life—is a story not of success, but of failure.

I don't have to look far for confirmation of this thesis. Casting an eye over my shelves, I note a collective narrative of lost chances, failed promise, unrealized dreams, from Melville's *Moby-Dick* to Gogol's "The Overcoat," that masterly tale of civil servants consumed by resentment and ambition; Gissing's *New Grub Street* and Thackeray's *Pendennis*, about journalists beaten into hacks; Stendhal's doomed hero, Julien Sorel, and Flaubert's Frédéric Moreau, who loses everything he loves. . . . How rarely such books tell of fulfillment, domestic harmony, hopes met. No, actually, they never do.

Even the success stories emerge from a chrysalis of failure. What stands out for me in the biographies of Faulkner and Fitzgerald are the months and years they wasted out in Hollywood, getting sodden over their squandered gifts. Cyril Connolly, one of the most distinguished critics of his day, made his name with a book, *Enemies of Promise*, that elegiacally bemoaned his lack of distinction. "In my late twenties and early thirties," writes the novelist Paul Auster in his memoir *Hand to Mouth*, "I went through a period of years when everything I touched turned to failure." Ah!

I'm so obsessed with this theme that I actually keep a "failure file." Let's see: Here's Norman Mailer, one of the greatest novelists of our time, summing up his legacy in an interview with the *New York Times*: "Part of the ability to keep writing over the years comes down to living with the expectation of disappointment. You just want to keep the store going. You're not going to do as well this year as last probably, but nonetheless let's keep the store going." If Norman Mailer feels this way about his achievement, imagine how the rest of us feel. And here's an article from the *Times*'s Arts & Leisure section called "Still Dreaming the Rock 'n' Roll Dream," about an aging rock star wannabe who's been trying to market a CD he recorded with his sister, a jewelry designer, in the basement of his Long Island home. "For thirty years, Andy Zwerling has epitomized the struggling musician, refusing to quit," reads the deck. "I think our time is now," the sister declares. Over Chinese food, Andy opens his fortune cookie: *You have the power to write your own future.* "Welcome to Andyland," he says wryly. Welcome to Everymanland.

Athletics is particularly fertile terrain. "All good sports reporters know that the best stories are in the loser's locker room," Pete Hamill observed in a review of *A Pitcher's Story,* Roger Angell's anatomy of David Cone's agonizing decline. In sports, failure is played out before our eyes. We get to *see* people fail. In an essay called "The Art of Failure," Malcolm Gladwell reviews two celebrated instances of "choking"—Jana Novotna's loss to Steffi Graf in a Wimbledon final where she was just five points away from victory, and Greg Norman's dramatic unraveling in a Masters golf tournament that saw him squander a six-stroke lead on the last day. "He had fumbled away the chance of a lifetime," writes Gladwell, narrating the catastrophe hole by hole. "Losers are more like the rest of us," observes Pete Hamill. "They make mistakes they can't take back."

How we torture ourselves over these mistakes. "You took a wrong turn," a legendary publisher said to me when I decided against writing the authorized biography of a famous American writer. The publisher was the author's literary executor and had invited me to write this book when I was thirty years old. It was a great honor, but I returned the advance money five years later and told him the job wasn't for me. I had some antipathy to the subject that I couldn't root out; the idea of spending a decade with him made my heart sink. The publisher warned me that I was making a mistake; and, as I stumbled through a succession of ill-advised jobs and book projects over the next decade, I could literally *hear* his voice as he uttered his somber prophecy. Why hadn't I listened?

Because you never do.

I want to go back and do it all over again, go back and do it right. In my mid-fifties, I begin to understand my strengths and weaknesses,

what I'm capable of and what I'm not. I'd make the right choices now—
I'd write the biography of the famous American writer; I wouldn't quit
the excellent job I had at the *New York Times* to go off and freelance. I
wouldn't, I wouldn't . . . Too late! Get over it. And anyway, who's to say
that I didn't in the end make the *right* choices—the decisions that, however much pain they caused me at the time, turned out to be the road to
freedom. Maybe I'd made those choices in part because I lacked self-
knowledge, and in part because I wanted something more. If I failed to
grasp the Golden Ring, at least I reached for it.

Lying awake one night rehearsing my litany of errors, I recall a
moment when I was forty and between assignments, between jobs. It
was ten o'clock on a weekday morning, and I sat at the counter of the
Three Brothers—or was it the Four Brothers?—coffee shop, staring out
the window at the stream of traffic storming by. Buses, delivery trucks,
taxis jounced over the rough pavement of Amsterdam Avenue. Everybody was on the way to somewhere, in a hurry, purposeful. The coffee
shop was nearly empty. In a corner sat an elderly woman reading the
Post, her cane leaning against the seat. Another booth was occupied by a
middle-aged man in a thin Windbreaker. He had long sideburns and
thick glasses; his hair was thinning in front. He was studying a letter,
reading it over and over. I stirred my coffee. My heart was a stone in my
chest. I had nothing to do. I thought: this is your life. You took a wrong
turn, missed the boat, bet the wrong horse. Blew it.

I walk down the street of a strange city at night and glimpse,
through a brightly lit window, a tableau of seeming harmony—a man
hunched over a desk, reading a book by the soft light of an Oriental
lamp. I'm seized with envy. What a perfect life is framed by that window! The man is a well-known writer, a journalist who's putting the last
touches on his weekly column for a prestigious journal of opinion; he's
just back from a lively dinner party, looking up a reference to Yeats . . . I

was making it up: for all I knew, he was an out-of-work accountant with a drinking problem; his wife wanted a divorce; his mother had just died; his son was into drugs. All of us, I suspect, imagine that a world exists from which we alone have been excluded; all of us have our noses pressed against the glass. But if we contemplate our own lives, not the phantom life on the other side, we might find things in them to envy— a family that's intact; a job we like; good health (the thing we take for granted and on which all happiness depends). Good fortune is there, however sporadic, however modest, however difficult to achieve; the trick is to recognize it.

On an unnaturally warm Sunday evening in the spring of 1986 (I can still recall the date: May 18), I left my apartment on the Upper West Side in quest of a Monday *New York Times*. I had learned that it would carry Christopher Lehmann-Haupt's make-or-break review of my first novel, a coming-of-age story about a Chicago Jewish boy in love with literature. There was a newsstand on the corner of Seventy-second Street and Broadway where you could get the next day's newspaper at eleven o'clock the night before—the "bulldog edition." At ten of eleven, I was loitering beneath the buzzing neon sign of Gray's Papaya, waiting for the bundle of papers to be thrown off the delivery truck. Minutes later, I stood reading Lehmann-Haupt's review with trembling hands while scraps of trash swirled around my feet. A thorough search among my papers turns up no trace of this review, or of Jonathan Yardley's even more vicious dismissal in the *Washington Post*. They must have been too painful to keep. But I can recite from memory the last phrase of Leslie Fiedler's demo job in the *Times Book Review:* he admitted that he'd laughed out loud, but he wasn't sure "who the joke was on." And I can also recite the conclusion of Sven Birkerts's assessment in the *New Republic*; alluding to a Joycean image in my novel of melted-winged

Icarus plunging from the sky, the kindly Birkerts concluded, "I fear he will not make it."

On the night of Lehmann-Haupt's verdict, I lay rigid in bed, listening to the angry horns of taxis down in the street. I was thirty-seven. It wasn't as if I hadn't failed before. When I was twenty-four, I had written a hundred pages of a novel about a strange, reclusive writer living in squalor on the North Side of Chicago and sent it to Ted Solotaroff, the editor of the much admired *New American Review;* I was delirious when he wrote back all but offering me a book contract. Could he just see another chapter or two before he got the go-ahead? Solotaroff was a god to me—writer of deep essays, friend of Philip Roth, occupant of the red-hot center of American literary life. Ecstatic, I hurried off to my neighborhood bar, the Plough & Stars, and downed a pint of Guinness. During the next few days, I knocked out the chapters that Solotaroff was eagerly awaiting. They came easily. Comic, J. P. Donleavy–like scenes involving the writer's dwarf uncle, a poetry-spouting mynah bird, and other picaresque details spilled forth from my electric typewriter. I dispatched the manuscript and waited for the good news, pacing up and down in my apartment like a madman out of Poe as I listened for the mail to drop through the slot each day. Finally, a fat envelope arrived. It contained my manuscript and a letter that read, "I'm sorry to have to write in this way, to deliver a bucket of cold water on a work in progress . . ." I had somehow gone off in a wrong direction, broken the spell I'd managed to create in my original submission, which captured the drab, wintry Chicago I really knew. I crawled under the dining-room table in my sparsely furnished apartment, curled up on the cold floor, and wept.

But to fail in your early twenties is of a different order of magnitude from failing in your late thirties. The day Lehmann-Haupt's punishing review came out, I sat in front of my computer screen all day, doggedly

pushing on with my work in progress—a novel about a struggling novelist in New York whose child almost dies of meningitis—and fielding
congratulatory phone calls from people who were impressed to see my
photograph in the paper and hadn't read the review. I knew that it was
important to keep going—to show Lehmann-Haupt that I wouldn't be
shut down. A few weeks later, I stopped in the middle of a sentence—
"Jesse's not breathing!"—and turned off my computer. I never wrote
another line of fiction.

Our belief in perpetual self-improvement goads us to go on to the
next thing in the name of "new challenges," even if doing so means
being promoted beyond our natural abilities or simply landing in the
wrong job (the foreign correspondent at the *Times* who becomes a
managing editor because that's how you climb the corporate ladder but
who hates administration; the distinguished critic who joins a glossy
newsweekly and discovers that she's no good at writing eight-hundred-
word reviews). The novel was supposed to be *my* next big thing, and
since my first published book, a biography of Delmore Schwartz, had
gotten favorable reviews, how could it not do well? The omens had been
good: an auction that netted a substantial advance; an announced first
printing of thirty thousand, and a glossy-looking galley for reviewers; a
lucrative sale to England. "I'm sure it will take off," I breezily informed
my parents, who of course were sure as well.

In the end, the novel sold six thousand copies; the rest got pulped.
It's not enough to say that I took it hard; it felt as if a death had
occurred—the death of hope. I saw myself as an outcast, my life as a
series of irretrievably squandered opportunities. In my journal I drew
up lists of "people who liked the book." A sample from these years:

*I was out of control, buying—for the first time in months—a pack
of Luckies, standing and smoking at a pizza counter.*

It's as if there's a wall of glass between me and people who are successful.

Things were going somewhat better for the last two days; then I heard that Ben Sonnenberg [the editor of Grand Street*] had a party last night to which we weren't invited, and it dawned on me—again—that I've utterly forfeited my place in the New York literary world.*

"Again" is right: the journal is a stupefyingly repetitious record of my refusal to grasp the deficiencies of my character and the limits of my talent; to recognize what I was (and wasn't); to value what I'd accomplished. I wasn't a novelist—that exalted, larger-than-life figure revered by generations of high school English teachers—but I had, with great difficulty and much persistence, become a writer.

Eventually, after a few years of therapy, I came out of my depression. I got a job that I liked; found a book that I wanted to write; and began to shed the tiresome self-pity that had tied me in knots for so long. At first, writing was slow work: I'd grown attached to the notion that failure was my irrevocable fate. But gradually I began to see my novelistic Waterloo for what it was. I remember a review of my Delmore Schwartz biography in which the reviewer said that the book was "peppy"—that it was less the work of a scholar than of someone who liked to talk on the phone with a cup of steaming coffee by his side. At the time, my feelings were hurt. Wasn't the reviewer saying, in a nice way, that I was a lightweight? Now I prefer to read it differently: the reviewer had simply been responding to my temperament—eager, energetic, more at home with interviews than with texts—as it revealed itself on the page. For better or worse, that was who I was.

I receive in the mail, forwarded from my English publishers, an invitation to a memorial service for Ian Hamilton, a British critic and poet with whom I had a slight—but to me significant—acquaintance. (We'd had lunch a few times.) It's to be held at the Polish Hearth Club in southwest London, offering "food, drink, music and football." I can't go over, but that night I raise a glass to Ian in my New York kitchen.

Why football? Because Ian often said, only half kidding, that he had really longed to be a professional soccer ("football" in England) player and had only settled for a literary career because he was sickly. A career is what he had: as a poet, Hamilton was distinctly—even aggressively—minor. His last collection, *Sixty Poems,* contained all the poems he ever published. "He was too interested in others to be a poet of realized reputation," suggested a reviewer of his last, posthumous book, *Against Oblivion,* brief biographical and literary portraits of forty-five contemporary poets. It was as a critic, a biographer (of Robert Lowell), and the founding editor of several literary journals, most notably *The New Review,* that Hamilton distinguished himself: "My technique was to start another magazine when things got hopeless." In a long interview in the *London Review of Books* just a month before he died of lung cancer at the age of sixty-three, he described his pursuit of the literary vocation as "conscientious service."

His personal life was messy, even by the standards of London literary journalists, legendary for their consumption of alcohol and disorderly sexual arrangements. He had several marriages, several mistresses, and several children, all of whom he supported on his modest wages. He was never photographed without a cigarette in his mouth and liked to say that he was sorry not to be able to smoke while he was asleep. At once clear-eyed and regretful about the "disappointed hopes" of the poets whose lives and works he chronicled with such tactful sympathy, he recognized—and forgave—their limitations, aware of the transience even of what little they managed to achieve. His regret about his own missed chances was encapsulated in a late poem called "Biography":

> *Who turned the page? When I went out*
> *Last night, his Life was left wide-open,*
> *Half-way through, in lamplight on my desk:*
> *The Middle Years.*
> *Now look at him. Who turned the page?*

In his last interview, Hamilton said, with classic English self-deprecation: "The poems I produced happened to be the only things I could do." *The only things I could do:* how much more I appreciate that line than I would have twenty years ago.

Shrinks

"**W**hat are you thinking?"

Dr. Bein (as I'll call him) always asked me this question after a minute or two of silence. I lay on the couch staring up at the ceiling. My head rested on a colorful embroidered pillow covered by a white hand-kerchief—presumably to protect it from the greasy heads of patients. It had often occurred to me to talk about this handkerchief, which annoyed me; it conveyed tacit criticism of my hygiene (though why hygiene should be singled out was an interesting question in itself; was I the only one who would soil his precious pillow?) But to bring up the issue would have been to gratify Dr. Bein. He was a shrewd psychiatrist, nimble at interpretation and familiar by now with the various feints and ruses I employed to deflect his probing. I had been seeing him off and on for six years, sometimes once a week (if I skipped or forgot an appointment, a regular occurrence), more often twice. On several occasions, I had pronounced myself cured or, anyway, sick of the process and had drifted off; but each time some new crisis in my life had brought me back. Dr. Bein had often tried to persuade me to go into analysis, to come four times a week instead of two; I, meanwhile, in the grip of a stubborn resistance, had been reluctant even to lie down on the couch. It had taken a full year for him to get me from my preferred position, sitting up in a chair and facing him—I'm not really in therapy, was the implication; I'm simply here for a fireside chat—to the prone position in which I now found myself, helpless, docile, prostrate (as I saw it), just another garden-variety neurotic droning on about his mother.

"I'm thinking about the handkerchief on this pillow," I finally mumbled.

"What about it?"

I could almost feel the force of Dr. Bein's attention. Like a hunting dog suddenly picking up the trail, he had leaned forward in his chair, his loafered foot levering up and down in my peripheral vision. In the air-conditioned basement room, the white-noise machine humming in the corner, he gave off an air of tense expectancy: here at last was material.

"I don't know," I answered sullenly. "Like, what's it for?"

"But I have many patients," Dr. Bein said.

"I'm aware of that," I retorted. "The question is: who are these people I see in the waiting room? They all seem so . . ." I groped for the word: "Depressed."

"What makes you think so?"

"Well, like that woman who comes in after me? The one with the sallow face? She's always eating something from a paper bag when I come out."

"And why does that bother you?"

I lay on the couch in silence, embarrassed by my desire to be my psychiatrist's only patient, the sole recipient of his attention. How easy I was to see through! How adept at rehearsing the old familiar themes that I'd cobbled together to form a story—what they call in psychiatry the "narrative."

Dr. Bein was not my first psychiatrist. When I was sixteen, my parents, perplexed by their moody child, who spent summer evenings sitting alone on a boulder overlooking Lake Michigan or closeted in his room writing poetry, had sent me to a child psychologist. I can't remember his name, but I have a distinct image of him: bearded, bespectacled, wearing a cardigan, lounging in a black leather chair. The room was crowded with Mexican artifacts and dusty plants. Why was I there? I ran with the artistic crowd—dope-smoking, cape-wearing, guitar-playing, Gauloises-smoking kids who wrote poetry and sat in their rooms listening to the cerebral musings of Thelonius Monk. On weekends we hung out at the No Exit café beneath the elevated tracks. We read *Siddhartha, Under the Volcano, The Way of Zen, Howl* in the chapbook-size City Lights edition. We took the el to Chicago and sat in the Clark Theatre all night watching Godard films. We shopped for our wardrobes at the Salvation Army store.

This cluster of behavioral tics concealed a potent cultural myth: artists were "maladjusted." It was the central myth of modernism, expressed in Edmund Wilson's *The Wound and the Bow* through the story of Philoctetes, whose incurable wound, the result of a snakebite on his foot, is compensated for by the magic bow in his possession, which never misses its mark: "The victim of a malodorous disease which renders him abhorrent to society and periodically degrades him and makes him helpless is also the master of a superhuman art which everyone has to respect and which the normal man finds he needs." I myself was saturated with this idea: one of the touchstones of my adolescence was Lionel Trilling's essay "Art and Neurosis" in *The Liberal Imagination,* which traced the connection between genius and the mental afflictions that produced it, from the romantics to Freud. The lesson Trilling's essay taught was that the artist is by nature sick: "He is what he is by virtue of his successful objectification of his neurosis." In other words, to be creative you have to be crazy.

The psychologist I saw in his comfortable Victorian house on a tree-lined street encouraged this connection. He wanted me to accept my difference, to be proud that I was "sensitive"—a "nonconformist," "other-directed," to borrow a then-popular term. Psychiatry, in this scheme of things, was less a means of cure than a credential: to be in treatment meant you were "talented."

Whatever my talent, it wasn't for therapy. After a few visits the psychologist gave up and referred me to a child psychiatrist in Chicago, Dr. Newman, who had an office lined with serious books—a complete edition of the works of Freud, row upon row of psychiatric journals, the novels of Thomas Mann, the Bollingen edition of Jung. His manner was professional, affable but firm. He was plump and worked in shirtsleeves, his tie askew, his suit jacket hung over a chair.

I was fond of Dr. Newman. I sat up in a chair, facing him—the psychologist had made me lie on the couch, pretending to psychoanalyze me—and talked about my problems. By my junior year in high school, I had wrecked my father's Buick and nearly gotten suspended from Evanston High School for disseminating an underground paper called *La Fuerza* (*The Force*).

"Let's work on this issue," Dr. Newman would say, focusing his kindly gaze on me. "Why do you think you get in trouble?"

"To get attention?"

"That's interesting." One of the things I liked about Dr. Newman was that he claimed to find everything I said "interesting." I, in turn, found his pudginess comforting. He smoked cigars, but not in a pompous way; he was messy, his white shirts smudged with cigar ash, and his lack of fastidiousness reassured me that he wasn't perfect. Many years later, when I came to read the work of Heinz Kohut, I recognized in Kohut's emphasis on the value of empathy the methods of Dr. Newman. It wasn't enough to understand the sources of your patient's suffering; you had to enter into it, experience it, feel it. I later learned that Kohut, who had fled Hitler's Vienna and ended up in Chicago, had an office in the same building, and that Dr. Newman had been one of his students.

The great unanswerable question about psychoanalysis, of course, is: does it work? I have a friend, a successful doctor, who is, by any standard, uncommonly sane: he has been in a strong marriage for twenty years, he radiates calm and good cheer, his children adore him; he's not angry at his parents. "What's his secret?" I once asked a mutual friend. "Joe's been shrunk," my friend answered. He put in a lot of couch time, and it worked. But in my experience Joe is the exception: just about everyone else I know has been in and out of therapy for years, with no visible results. On the other hand, who's to say what would have happened if we *hadn't* been in therapy? We might have ended up like the literary generation on which I aspired to model myself until I realized I didn't have the stamina for it—the writers who drank their way through multiple marriages, slept with everyone in sight, and eventually dropped dead of smoking or wore out their hearts, all in the belief that talent was a license to misbehave.

I myself clung for a long time to the myth that neurosis and creativity were linked—and was abetted in it by a psychiatrist I'll call Lowell Edmunds, who followed Dr. Newman in the line of therapeutic succession. Dr. Edmunds was my "college" psychiatrist; I went to see him in my freshman year, after I failed introduction to philosophy. Surrounded by all those valedictorians with 800 SATs, I couldn't handle the pressure. I wondered if I should just go home, enroll at the local junior college, read the *Norton Anthology of English Verse* at the Formica-topped desk where I had once labored over my high school homework, the fake-bronze tennis trophies on a shelf overhead, the White Sox pennant on the wall.

"I think you're being a trifle histrionic," Dr. Edmunds said on the first day, after I'd laid out this scenario in his office on the ground floor of a gray-shingled town house a few blocks from campus. He leaned back in his chair, a Doral held languidly between his fingers. Tall and lanky, he wore gold-rimmed glasses; his hair, as silken as a badger's, was brushed back from his forehead in the old-fashioned way. He had a habit of leaning back in his Eames chair, head cocked, long legs stretched out before him and crossed at the ankle, eyes nearly shut against the smoke that curled from his cigarette, as if he were about to fall asleep—which, in truth, he often did. I would be confessing unseemly thoughts—the usual patient routine—when I would suddenly notice that Dr. Edmunds's eyes were closed. He was breathing lightly, rhythmically; his chest rose and fell. At first, when this happened, I would lie quietly on the couch, afraid of disturbing him. As the silence deepened, a signal would go off somewhere in his unconscious, alerting him that he was in the midst of a session, and he would start awake, opening his eyes wide in surprise.

At last there came a time when, emboldened by the autonomy that my psychiatrist was supposed to be laboring to instill in me, I would, at the first indication that he was about to nod off, call out sharply, "Dr. Edmunds!" Upon which he would fling himself forward in his chair, shake his head like a dog trotting out of the ocean, and mutter a low "uhmmmm." Looking back now, I could make the case that his dozing was inadvertently therapeutic: it was a way of instructing me that my monologues were soporific, that I should knock it off, stop whining, get on with my life. Or maybe he was just sleepy.

"I hear everything you say," the doctor insisted when I finally brought up the matter of his persistent somnolence. "I don't miss anything of importance."

"*Of importance?* How do you know what's important and what

isn't?" I protested. From then on, Dr. Edmunds struggled manfully to stay awake during our sessions, rejecting my suggestion that I come earlier in the day when he was more alert. I tried to be more interesting, injecting a note of urgency into my discourse. Even so, the doctor dozed.

Dr. Edmunds's office was a prelapsarian nicotine Eden; every ten minutes we'd both whip out our packs, the ashtray on the table beside my chair already brimming with butts from previous patients. I smoked some foul English brand called Half & Half, a mixture of pipe and cigarette tobacco. When I expressed concern about the health issue—it was already five years since the surgeon general's report, and the lethality of smoking was no longer conjectural—Dr. Edmunds waved a dismissive hand; I could deal with that issue later, he suggested, once I'd sorted out the source of my psychic pain. Meanwhile, we both sat puffing away like the dogs in cancer experiments.

Dr. Edmunds was a Freudian, I suppose, in the sense that all psychiatrists were Freudian in those days: that is, they believed that character was formed in the crucible of childhood, by the behavior of one's parents. Thus did Oedipal conflicts, the maternal introject, a dominating father, play themselves out in the theater of infantile sexuality; thus did the child's anal fixations determine the course of the adult's sexuality. I was in treatment with him on and off through my college years, with little abatement of my unhappiness. Its causes, in retrospect, were unremarkable—I was lonely; my girlfriend had left me; *The New Yorker* had turned down my poems—but the intensity of pain these tribulations kindled was no small thing at the time. I remember a desolate weekend my senior year. It was a Saturday afternoon, and the streets were eerily quiet; it felt as if the entire campus was at the football game. I sat at the table in my tiny apartment, furnished with Danish-modern castoffs from my parents, and wondered how, in my pursuit of a phantom independence, my determination to enact the paradigm of the artist as Other, a figure out of *Notes from Under-*

ground, a tortured soul for whom the literary vocation was a sentence, a self-imprisonment, I had managed to isolate myself so thoroughly from the vivifying world of classes and nights watching *Casablanca* with a gang of friends in the local "art film" theater.

In desperation, I called up Dr. Edmunds and made an emergency appointment. We met an hour later in his office. I cried and cried. Dr. Edmunds, however, made no effort to soften his therapeutic strategy of detachment. He sat scrutinizing me through his rimless spectacles, a naturalist observing some curious species he had just stumbled across in the rain forest; I could almost see him in a pith helmet and khaki shorts.

In the end, I pulled myself together largely on my own. I found a new girlfriend, moved into a funky Victorian house with some classmates I liked, got on with my life. To this day, I don't know why. Maybe the phrase "mental weather" should be taken literally: one day a storm, the next day sunshine. When I graduated at the end of that year, I left behind Dr. Edmunds as well. I didn't hear from him for quite a few years—two decades in fact. One day a letter appeared in my mail cubby at the *New York Times,* addressed in a familiar spidery hand that I recognized instantly from the bills that used to arrive each month with the number of consults and the all-purpose diagnosis of "anxiety." So he was alive!

I still have the letter. "Dear Mr. Atlas" it began—Dr. Edmunds prided himself on his formality; he wasn't one to make the doctor/therapist relationship more intimate by putting it on a first-name basis. He had read my work over the years and had often meant to write me. "But I gave in to inertia each time, usually because I was in total agreement and hence had little to add." Why, then, was he writing to me now? I had just published a colicky essay in a national magazine in which I confessed that certain canonical books—most notably the work of Henry James and Faulkner—bored me. Not only did I question the obeisance paid to the Great Books, but I wondered aloud how many people actually got all the way through some of the brick-size novels that have been promoted to the status of classics. It was an ill-advised outburst—even the editor asked me if I really wanted to go through with it—and I shouldn't have been surprised by the public outcry. My former psychiatrist, not surprisingly, was among the critics; he "deplored" the piece and was writing to let me know how he felt.

Dr. Edmunds's literary affectations had always enraged me. He once gave me an essay he'd written—in itself a breach of the transference. The only thing I remember about it was that it was laced with allusions to Coleridge and Dr. Johnson, and that it made reference to Wallace Stevens's poem "Forty-Seven Ways of Looking at a Blackbird"—only Dr. Edmunds got the number wrong.

"It's '*Thirteen* Ways,' not Forty-seven," I had blurted at my next session, almost before I'd settled into my chair, so eager was I to correct his gaffe. He frowned. "I must have somehow conflated Stevens's number with Heinz Fifty-seven varieties," he offered lamely.

A quarter of a century later, nothing had changed. He was still name-dropping writers. "I can agree with you fully about Faulkner," Dr. Edmunds asserted in his letter, "but not about James, whom I began in high school when wild hawthorn was blossoming on the fringes of the Skokie Marsh." *Wild hawthorn* indeed.

The letter was signed "with warmest regards," but the damage was done: I was furious. The instant I finished Dr. Edmunds's letter, I sat down at my computer like Glenn Gould attacking a Bach piano sonata and dashed off a furious reply.

Dear Dr. Edmunds:

How interesting it was that you read my work for so many years but managed to refrain from acknowledging your awareness of it with a letter or even a note—a gesture that would have meant so much to me. Only when you had a disagreement with something I'd written could you overcome your "inertia."

By coincidence, I have meant to write you all these years, but was impeded by a similar inertia. What I wanted to say was this: at a vulnerable period in my life, when I lacked the resources to think for myself and relied on you to help me find my way, you fell asleep in sessions, fatally undermining my self-confidence. And do you remember the time you sat there impassively when I came in for an emergency appointment one Saturday and evinced no sympathy—going by the book in your determination to maintain a psychiatric neutrality?

I was just getting warmed up: in successive paragraphs I outlined how his failure to address these issues had caused me such unhappiness at that time in my life.

"I was surprised & deeply distressed to hear what a painful experience you had in psychotherapy with me, & how oblivious I had been of what you were feeling," Dr. Edmunds replied with admirable promptitude and frankness (employing, I noticed, ampersands that gave his prose a "literary" touch. Who did he think he was? Ezra Pound?)

Obviously I cannot defend myself or make amends for the past, but, for whatever it's worth, I can tell you how I recalled your therapy. My memories are of a lively, continuously interesting process in which your verbal skills & a highly developed capacity for self-understanding made my interpretations almost unnecessary. I don't think of myself as the stereotypical silent analyst of that era, but as allowing your insights to unfold. About dozing during a session, I can only wish you had called it to my attention.

A little late. And if his interpretations were unnecessary, why was I paying to sit babbling in his office when I could just as easily have confided in my brother or an old girlfriend? But my anger ebbed as suddenly as it arrived. He'd acknowledged his failings. At this point in my life, I was intimately familiar with error—give the guy a pass. I wrote back a conciliatory reply. Again Dr. Edmunds responded at once. This time he apologized for his "defensiveness" about dozing off: "As you can imagine, you weren't the only patient who had that problem."

I could just picture Dr. Edmunds shuffling about his book-lined office in leather slippers and shaking his head: *Why did I ever write that maniac?*

Years later, I had left a succession of jobs with impulsive haste and ended up at a newsweekly that required me to write obits of celebrated sitar players and Japanese lingerie tycoons. Assigned to do a "service" piece on where to find the best deals in summer suits—by the way, what was so bad about that?—I walked out of the office at nine o'clock on a hot August night, after a late "close," and stood on Sixth Avenue, inhaling bus fumes in the muggy, grit-thick air. The "top editor" of the section had rewritten the piece sentence by sentence while I sat beside him like a slow student being walked through a geometry problem by a grumpy teacher. When he was done, he handed my copy back to me without looking up, already preoccupied with the next piece on his desk. I couldn't—wouldn't—learn how to do it.

I called the New York Psychoanalytic Institute for a referral, and the rest is therapy. Enter Dr. Bein. He was physically unprepossessing, but as tough as a drill sargeant. "You're secretive," he would say when I clammed up rather than confessing my latest misdeed. "When are you going to ask yourself why you do the things you do?"

A good question. The whole point of therapy, I was to learn over the next few years, was simply that: to ask yourself what you were doing, and why; to make sure that it was what you wanted to do; and if it wasn't, not to do it. But getting there wasn't quite so simple.

My "resistance"—the official psychiatric term for the fire wall of obfuscation that patients erect between themselves and their therapists—was fierce. Our skirmishes over the issue of lying down on the couch were symptomatic. After a year or so, I did lie down—gingerly at first, like a yogi on a bed of nails—then, as the advantage of not having to keep up social rituals (eye contact, gestures, expressions) began to manifest itself, with enthusiastic assent. Lying down enabled me to concentrate on the question Dr. Bein posed whenever I was silent—"So, what are you thinking?"—without having to think about what *he* was thinking.

The trick was to be candid, to let the unconscious have its way; but learning to do that was as hard as learning to play the piano. You had to practice. You had to want to be good at it. Dr. Bein was unsentimental; he gave little encouragement. Yet he was no strict Freudian either, stonily silent and withholding; he greeted me in a friendly way and actually seemed glad to see me. At the end of the hour—or fifty minutes, to be precise—he would mention that our time was up in a voice that almost seemed tinged with regret. And he didn't nod off either.

The hardest thing to figure out was also the most basic: is anything happening here? Week after week, month after month, I lay on the couch in Dr. Bein's concrete bunker—the basement of the town house he owned—and did battle with my demons, raging against mama, papa, big brother, boss, above all Dr. Bein himself, the slight and compact figure who had become, through the magic of transference, the biggest obstacle of all—an army of largely phantom enemies impeding my journey to grown-uphood. Dr. Bein wasn't of the passive school. Just when I was beginning to gather a head of steam, he would interject some withering commentary: "But why do you let him do it?" "Maybe you don't want to write that book."

Dr. Bein's deft but relentless probing of my motives elicited in me a wish to fend him off. By what right did he sit there and issue pronouncements? But in therapy you had to trust the therapist. And if the therapist should turn out to be just an ordinary person with a modest potbelly and a height that put him an inch below his already short analysand, that was okay. And if it should turn out that the doctor's furnishings—nondescript contemporary art, African statues, macramé rugs—reminded the patient of the interiors of his relatives' houses back in Chicago, or that the doctor forgot the name of the girl with red hair that the patient had been fixated on in third grade, the guy was only human.

After a few years of lying on Dr. Bein's couch combing through every trivial detail of the day—my childhood, my dreams, my fantasies—I was as tuckered out as a child after a long day at the zoo. I wanted my two afternoons a week back, and the money I spent on psychoanalysis. Above all, I wanted freedom—freedom from myself. Not everything can be cured. Life deals out its daily dose of hurt. I'd had my fill of insight.

In a fit of self-confidence, I terminated Dr. Bein. From time to time I was tempted to call him, as if he were an old lover, just to check in; but I generally resisted. For one thing, no lover charges you for a visit. (Dr. Bein had kept an eagle eye on my income and uncannily knew or sensed whenever it went up, giving him a mandate to increase his fee.) Once or twice, under the pressure of events, I actually made an appointment and went to see him. I sat across from him—no more lying down; I was here for a "consultation"—and filled him in on recent events, as casual as a guest on Letterman. He nodded and smiled. At the end of the hour—it had been whittled down to forty-five minutes now—he said, "So where would you like to go from here?" The answer was: home, back to work, anywhere *but* here. I was as curious as ever about how the mind worked, and about what could be learned from the analytic study of its contents. But did I want to stretch out on the couch twice a week and ruminate aloud about the transgressions, stumbles, errors, feints at self-sabotage, and idiotic blurts that informed a regular day? Did I want—again—to rehearse the parental misdeeds that had, in my ever-inventive imagination, hindered and distorted my passage to full adulthood? ("My father kicked me in the rear when I wouldn't wear my suit to cousin Irving's bar mitzvah.") No.

And yet life wouldn't let up. Depression is like an illness—it *is* an illness. It comes out of nowhere, seizes you in its grip, and drives out all happy memories. When you're in this condition you look back on your life and remember only the bad parts. You pass a park where you used to go with Molly when she was a child and you remember not those sun-filled mornings but how you heard one day about a promotion you didn't get and had to go take Molly to the park anyway. Pushing her on the swings, you were overcome by an exhaustion so deep that you longed for nothing more than to lie down in the damp grass and not wake up for a long time. When you're depressed, that's the day you remember. You pick up a magazine you once wrote for, producing pieces that found a wide and appreciative readership—and think of the piece that you worked on for six months that was rejected and how it felt to get the phone call from the editor. ("I'm really sorry to have to tell you this, Jim . . .") It's as if the other stuff never happened. The way you feel now is the way you have always felt and will always feel. That is depression.

I tried to assign reasons for these moods, to construct new narratives that would explain them. I pored over Kohut's key work, *The*

Analysis of the Self, using it as a therapeutic handbook, a way of treating myself. His insistence on regarding the patient's "demands for attention and admiration" as needs to be acknowledged was somehow bracing: instead of allocating blame, assigning causes to my pervasive sense of deprivation, I struggled to assert my dominion over it. Our behavior, Kohut believed, was in the end "beyond the law of motivation, i.e., beyond the law of psychic determinism." How I longed to believe this, to arrive at a belief in free will.

I consulted a cognitive therapist. In cognitive therapy, the "narrative" is irrelevant; the point is to identify and root out "dysfunctional thoughts," focusing on a patient's thought processes rather than attempting to treat symptoms through the painstaking reconstruction of traumas suffered in early life. One attractive feature of this "therapeutic modality," as variants on the practice of psychotherapy were called, was its brevity: a course of treatment generally consisted of eight or ten sessions, each an hour long, and then you were up and out. It either worked or it didn't. The therapist I went to swore that it did. "I have seen hundreds, thousands of people changed by this method," he said on my first visit.

Dr. Bergman's office was on the top floor of a nondescript medical building on the Upper East Side. When I knocked on his door, he opened it promptly and thrust out a hand. "Come in! Sit down!" His voice was warm, his manner direct. He gave me an appraising stare and motioned to a plain upholstered couch. He had a trim, clipped beard and horn-rimmed glasses. His suit was tan, well tailored but not sharp; its crisp fit contributed to his air of authority. He spoke with a soft guttural accent—Israeli, perhaps?

"So." He smiled, gazing at me as if I were a long-lost cousin just arrived from the Old Country. We were *landsmen,* sturdy pioneers in the New World of sanity. "What brings you here?" The implication was that we had practical business to deal with: let's roll up our sleeves and go to work! Stripped of its romantic literary connotations, my still-undiagnosed malady was now perceived to be a nuisance, an impairment to be treated like any physical trait—a stutter, a twitching eyelid, an inflammation of the sinuses.

Dr. Bergman listened to my Everyman's tale of neurotic woe, cocked his head, and looked me over. "We will see what we can do," he said and proceeded to explain, with a clarity and passion that instantly won me over, how cognitive therapy worked. "The brain has pathways, grooves. You have a thought, and this leads to another thought. If you can arrest this process at the very beginning, when you are just setting off down the familiar path that you're not even aware of, then you can say, 'Okay, so I have this feeling. How does it begin?' "

Dr. Bergman gave me homework: I was supposed to keep a "Dysfunctional Thoughts Record," a chart in which I recorded the vicissitudes of my moods in order to chart their etiology. The chart had five categories: Situation, "the actual event, stream of thoughts, daydream or recollection—leading to unpleasant emotion"; Emotions, in which I was supposed to specify whether I was "sad, anxious, etc."; Automatic Thoughts, which required me to "write thoughts or images that went through your mind" and then to rate my belief in these thoughts—i.e., how true I thought they were—from 1 to 100; Rational Responses, asking me to identify my "cognitive distortions" and to pose "alternative/rational responses"; and finally Outcome, in which I was invited to "rate belief in automatic thoughts."

Goal-oriented as always, I threw myself into the project of monitoring and dissecting my patterns of thought, writing them down in a journal every morning. It made for grisly reading: "Sinking mood in the morning—fretting about unreturned phone call from X . . . got depressed eating Chinese food . . . fear of what will happen when I'm old . . ." Within a few weeks, I began to get the hang of it. If you had a negative thought, your conscious mind was supposed to pounce on it like a defensive lineman tackling a quarterback as he sprinted for the goal, knocking out the "cognitive distortion" before it could establish itself, or—to preserve the metaphor—score.

Dr. Bergman reminded me of my fourth-grade flute teacher, Mr. Margolick, who used to interrupt as soon as I hit a false note, wagging his finger at me and chanting "uh-uh-uh-uh." When I got it right, he would exhale with a satisfied "ahhh." Now when I handed in my homework, Dr. Bergman would glance over it rapidly and fix me with his affectionate eyes, as if to say, *You see how easy it is?*

When I showed up for my eighth session, the conversation—for that's what it was—lagged: after twenty minutes, I'd run out of things to say, and so had Dr. Bergman. At his suggestion, I turned to my "dysfunctional thoughts" chart and began to read what I thought was the latest entry. It sounded familiar. Gradually the realization came over me: I'd read this exercise before.

I was done.

When I proposed to Dr. Bergman that perhaps I had come to the end of my course of treatment, he readily agreed. We talked in a desultory way until the end of the session. "It has been a pleasure," he said, leaping to his feet. We shook hands, and I walked out the door.

As I descended in the elevator, I remembered a joke: a guy walks out on his porch and sees a snail on the step. He picks it up, examines it briefly, then hurls it into the woods. For a year, two years, the snail toils through leaves and dirt and snow, inching his way back toward the porch. He makes his way up the stairs in his snail-like way, dragging his shell behind him until at last, half-dead, he reaches his destination. Just at that moment, the man who'd flung him into the woods opens his door and steps out onto the porch. The snail looks up at him and says, "What was that all about?"

My mind was now rational, or so it appeared to me. I was able to banish thoughts, arrest their course before they started off down the road to self-recrimination. Only I still didn't feel quite right. Depression continued to descend without warning, like a cloud-darkening sky.

A friend referred me to a famous psycho-pharmacologist. Dr. Pinsker, as I'll call him, worked out of a sparsely furnished office in a Midtown high-rise. The more streamlined the psychoanalytic method, I noticed, the more barren the office. Soon they'd have drive-through shrink outlets, the doctor sitting behind a plate-glass window with one of those headpiece microphones like a Burger Chef cashier: "Two Zoloft, a Prozac, and a Paxil to go."

The message of Peter Kramer's eloquent book *Listening to Prozac* was that the self was protean. The infusion of what were officially known as "seratonin reuptake inhibitors"—Prozac and the family of drugs that were being prescribed in ever greater numbers for depression—had so profound an effect on those who took them as to put in question the fundamental issue of who they were. These drugs weren't just mood altering; they were character altering. What Kramer called "cosmetic psycho-pharmacology" was in fact more than skin-deep; pills were now capable of transforming our very identities, making us into different people. What used to be considered character traits were now symptoms: from *character is fate* to *character is chemical*.

Dr. Pinsker had me fill out a form—so many forms!—checking off my level of various symptoms and emotions, from one to ten: anger, insomnia, depression. "You should have a box for envy," I said.

His face lit up. "That's a good idea." He studied my form while I sat across from his empty desk, then asked me a few questions about my psychiatric history. Dr. Pinsker listened impassively. "What blows me away is that no one ever sorted this out," he said when I got to the end. He gave me a searching look that made me uneasy. Was there some underlying condition he'd stumbled upon in the course of our interview? Was I much worse off than I realized? It even occurred to me, in a fit of madness, that he had pressed a button concealed beneath his desk, like a bank teller in the midst of a holdup, summoning a team of hospital orderlies who would burst in with a straitjacket and hustle me off to Bellevue.

But no, he was just trying to figure out what drugs to prescribe and their dosage. "Your moods go up and down." He drew a jagged graph in the air with his finger.

"Why?" I asked.

Dr. Pinsker shrugged. "Who knows?" He scribbled on a piece of paper and handed it to me. "Take two of these a day for a week, and then go down to one. Take one of these every other day. Take one of these and one of these . . ." He tapped on his desk. "Call me for an appointment in two weeks."

Two weeks later, I was back in Dr. Pinsker's office. "How goes it?" he said.

"Miraculous." I described how calm I felt—relaxed, at ease with myself, full of purpose. I was working well; I'd lost weight; I slept at night. Dr. Pinsker listened for a while, lolling back in his chair, hands clasped behind his head. All at once, he shot forward and stared at me intently.

"Do you wear collar stays?" he said.

"What?" I responded incredulously.

"Do you wear collar stays?" he said again, more firmly this time. "There's something wrong with your collar."

I reached up and felt it. Sure enough, the collar was loose; in my hurry, I'd forgotten to put in the little plastic spears that I kept in a wooden tray on my dresser. "Uh, I usually do," I answered.

"Let me give you a tip," Dr. Pinsker said, fumbling in a desk drawer. "You know those plastic keys they give you now in hotels?" He fished one out of a drawer and held it up for me to see. "I collect these on business trips. All you need is a scissors . . ." He found one in the drawer. "Any scissors will do." As he explained his method, he snipped away at the plastic rectangle like a kindergarten teacher showing a student how to make a paper necklace. "Like so," he announced proudly, holding up a spear-shaped approximation of a collar stay.

On the way out, I stopped in front of a mirror and inserted the collar stays Dr. Pinsker had fashioned. I paid for collar stays? I thought; but I didn't really mind. His advice was more practical than any I'd gotten from my other therapists.

I liked our visits. Dr. Pinsker was sympathetic, a good listener, and didn't pretend to know more than he did. I went to see him from time to time—"going in for a tune-up," a friend of mine who's a long-term but now-intermittent analysand calls it. "Some of this is just your nature," the doctor said at one of our sessions when I complained that I was down again. "You've done a lot, you've had a good life—not without disappointment like everyone else, not without pain, but a good life. The way you feel isn't always in your control. Your job is to know who you are and accept it—to be in your own nature." Drugs can only accomplish so much, he cautioned. In the end, you have to go it alone, figure out by yourself who you are. *Be in your own nature.*

A few days later, I stood at the window of my apartment at dusk, looking out over the vast cityscape, the horns of taxis rising up through the summer air. There was a spot on the carpet that depressed me; my bank account was seven hundred dollars overdrawn. I felt myself going down. I was reminded of the dialogue cloud over Charlie Brown: no words, just a tangle of black swirls.

I described to Dr. Pinsker the mysterious plummeting of mood I'd experienced as I stared out the window of my apartment in the dusk. "There was no reason; nothing had gone wrong. It just came over me."

He thought for a minute. "Do you have an iPod?" he said.

"An iPod?" I'd gotten Will one for his birthday. It was a fifth the size of a Walkman and could fit in your breast pocket. The earphones nestled in your ear like a hearing aid. "My son has one," I answered in bafflement.

"You should get one for yourself," Dr. Pinsker said. "They're unbelievable mood enhancers." He got up and walked over to the corner of his office. There, in a cradle, was the device. He fiddled with it for a minute, and the overture of *Rigoletto* flooded the room. Dr. Pinsker smiled. "Isn't that incredible? Listen to the sound! It's like having a stereo in your head. Three hundred dollars. You just download your CDs onto it. It fits over a thousand songs."

"An iPod," I repeated.

"Listen," he said, great intensity in his voice. "If you get one you can bring it in, leave it for twenty-four hours, and I'll download my music onto it. I won't charge you."

I went straight from his office to Radio Shack, purchased an iPod, and left it with his receptionist. The next day, when I came in to retrieve it, the door to Dr. Pinsker's office was open. I peeked in and he jumped up, ripping the tiny earphones off his head. I could see that he was in an excited state. He hurried over to the corner, unfastened my iPod from the cradle, and pressed it into my palm. "Go on, try it." He showed me how to select what I wanted to hear by rotating the dial with my finger. "You can do it by artists, by songs, by albums—whatever you want. It's all in alphabetical order."

I peered into the tiny window and rotated the dial as he'd demonstrated, scrolling down the list of titles on the tiny screen: Bach, Cello Concertos 5 and 6; Mozart, *Le Nozze di Figaro*; Vivaldi, *Four Seasons*. Dr. Pinsker clapped me on the shoulder. "You'll be amazed."

I stuffed a plastic earpiece in each ear while I was still descending in the elevator. In the lobby, I fiddled with the dial until I found *Rigoletto*, and pushed through the revolving door.

The music exploded in my head, a rush of sound beating against my skull. I could hear each note, each vibration of each cello, a massive injection of sound expanding, pouring through me as I floated down the street. It was Midtown Manhattan at rush hour, crowds jostling me on the jammed sidewalk, but I heard none of it. All I heard was Verdi.

The Body

2003

The ball is past my racket before I even see it.

"Forty-love," Will calls across the net. I trot over to the ad court and crouch, eyes glued to the ball as he gets ready to toss. It's in the air, I'm following it, it's here! This time I manage to get my racket on it but frame it and send it high in the air like a foul pop-up. It lands two courts down, where a doubles game is in progress, four cranky old guys in long pants. "Court six!" I yell. "Court six!" I wave my racket, and one of the guys retrieves the ball and sends it back to me—court eight—across a court where a man and woman play patty-cake, pushing the ball at each other.

"Five-one," William says.

This is the first year he's beaten me consistently. Last year we were about even. For the few years before that I had to finely calibrate the score, rigging a loss after I took a few games, careful not to throw the match too obviously but reluctant to frustrate him. Before that I stood at midcourt and volleyed the ball back at him. Before that I stood at the net and tossed it to him; he could barely hold the child's racket and had to swing at the ball with all his might to get it over. He's two inches taller than me now and serves at a hundred miles an hour, his body corkscrewing as he hammers the ball downward.

My serve. I bounce the ball three times, cock my racket, toss and swing. Bam! The return is down the line and out of reach. The next return, though, isn't quite as hard, and it's down the middle   right at me. I jump away and wave my racket at the ball in a toreador motion. It pings back deep to Will's backhand; he leaps high in the air, unleashes his two-handed swing, and cranks it down the line. But I've anticipated and I'm there. It's a defensive game I play against him nowadays; I'm satisfied just to get the ball back. I last for two more exchanges before he finishes me off with a huge overhead.

I play my best against this rangy boy. Knowing I can't win relaxes me. Competitive as ever, I scramble and flail, hoping to gain advantage by waiting him out. He's only sixteen, emotionally immature, right? It's only a matter of time before he cracks. But he doesn't. Battle-hardened by all the tournaments I've driven him to, all the clinics he's attended, he focuses his attention on each point, shrugging off errors—if he nets the ball or hits it long, never mind. On to the next. I'm the one who's getting frustrated. It feels weird to have the racket nearly knocked out of your hand, to find yourself sprinting away from overheads just to get out of the way. When he blasts a cross-court topspin forehand deep into the back court, I can only stand and admire it, and from a considerable distance at that.

Five–forty. Double set point. I get my first serve in, flat, the way you were taught to hit in my day, just knicking the service line. Will can't handle it and hits it long. Thirty-forty. On the next point, I miss my first serve. I don't have a second serve and have to dump the ball into the court—a big problem, as it turns out. Will steps into the ball and lashes it down the line with that newfangled swing, the grip a half-twist from the way I hold it, more like a backhand than a forehand. I slap at it feebly, but it's way out of reach. That's that.

I trudge to the net, and we shake hands. "I'll get you next time," I say.

Will gives me a searching look. "Actually, not."

Losing to Will is a confusing experience. On the one hand, I'm proud. It's a thrill to watch him trounce me, in physical and mental command of the game. I observe the grisly spectacle with detachment, as if I'm on the sidelines. When he hits a terrific shot, I cry out "Yes!" and pump my fist. But then I think: wait a minute. The guy's your opponent.

Day after day when he's around in the summer, I drag him away from his Xbox and make him play for two hours. It's like hitting against a backboard. Six-one, 6–2, 6–3. Once in a while I push him to 7–5; and one day when it's cool enough so that I don't wilt—and Will's off his game—I fight my way to a tiebreak. At 6–6, he looks across the net at me and mutters, "That's enough." I hit a decent serve and he jumps on it, smashing a winner cross-court. It's his serve. He steps up to the line, examines the ball in his hand. Bounce, bounce, bounce. Toss. Ace.

Will strides to the net and extends his hand. I put my arm around him and tousle his hair. "Nice game, Will."

Jerk.

When I play against the regulars in Vermont, there's no ambivalence. I want to win. On a blazing August day, we're battling it out on the public courts: Ed, Ron, Harry, and I. Our collective age approaches the 250 mark.

"Good!"

Ed has just played a ball that was clearly out, at least two inches wide of the alley, dumping it into the net as he made the call. Why did he do that? We're down 4–1 against Ron and Harry and don't have points to give away. But Ed is such a sweet man that he simply didn't have the heart to call Ron's shot out. I try not to countermand his generous calls; we're gentlemen here, or at least try to be. But it's hard not to cry, "For Chrissake, Ed, that was out by a mile."

We're playing early to avoid the heat. The court is dappled with shadows from the trees that surround the court, a lush green wall. But I'm already breathing hard, and we've only been out for half an hour. I can feel the effect of the hard surface on my knees. During the changeovers, I gulp from my water bottle and swab my face with a towel. Fortunately Ed has invested in folding canvas chairs this year, and we ease ourselves down for a minute or two, chatting about our kids and—in Ron's case—grandchildren. We've been playing together for so many years that I can track our advancing decline by the paraphernalia we now require: knee bands, gauze bandages wrapped around our wrists, ointments and salves. The posts beside the net resemble a surgical ward.

We split the first two sets and struggle on to a third. We're tiring rapidly; my first serve now has the velocity of what used to be my second serve. Down 6–5, Ed and I whisper near the fence; should we both rush net? Harry, in his seventies, has a damaged shoulder and can't lift the racket over his head to serve. He tosses the ball up, grabs the handle of his racket with both hands, and swings like a baseball coach hitting fungoes. He manages to get it over and never double-faults, but it's a weak serve, and easy to return. We decide to go for it—a risk. Harry's a shrewd player—he spends the winters down in Florida. He misses nothing at net, and throws a canny arsenal of stuff at us: down-the-line slices, drop shots, floating lobs. Racing back in a burst of speed that surprises me, I retrieve one over my head, like a Willie Mays basket catch, and send it high in the air, but alas, short—Harry handles it with dispatch, putting away a forehand volley. I stand at the back of the court, bent over, hands on knees, gasping for air.

We're befuddled and can't keep score. Harry calls out, "Forty–thirty?" "No, thirty–forty." He shakes his head. "That can't be. There was the serve you hit into the net, Ed's missed overhead . . ." He tries to remember the third point they won. "You hit one wide, and then there was the ball that hit the fence . . ." I can't remember the decisive point either. We stand at the net, conferring as solemnly as the leaders of the European Economic Union around a table in Geneva. Finally the answer to our stalemate comes to me: Ron netted a volley. The score is 30–40. Overexcited, I hit a backhand return of Harry's soft serve three feet out. Deuce. Ed also blasts one long. Now it's up to me to keep us in the game. I dance behind the service line, eager to powder the ball; I feel the nervous energy coursing through me. Lately, to calm myself, I've taken to inhaling deeply and breathing out while my opponent gets ready to serve. I'm oppressed by the responsibility; I've got to return serve or we lose. Harry floats it over. A backhand: damn. I hurry my swing and angle the ball downward into the net. In my head, I hear the cry of Charlie Brown on the mound as he launches a fastball into the stands: arrghh!

Game, set, and match. We gather at the net and shake hands all around. Our opponents look happy. Win or lose, it was a good game. And me? How can I describe the desolation that collects in my chest as I stow away my rackets?

So why do I do it? Why do I labor so, panting, lunging, retrieving? At one point I crash into the wire-mesh fence in a vain effort to return one of Harry's lobs. Why? To prove to myself that I'm strong, that there's still some vestige left of the body that loped from corner to corner on the cracked asphalt courts at Evanston High School when I played second doubles on varsity—the bottom of the ladder, but glad to be on the team at all. I want to feel the familiar joy of cracking the ball low over the net, passing my crouched opponent with a forehand down the line.

Ed claps me on the shoulder, a warmhearted and forgiving man: "You did well. We'll get 'em next time." He drapes his sopping terry cloth around his neck and trots off the court.

I get in my car and drive home enfolded in a gloomy silence. Van Morrison is in the CD player, ready to snap me out of it, but I've got brooding to do. What happened on that last point, the fatal backhand service return? Why didn't I get my racket back, move my feet, stay down?

I need help. I reach out to a tennis instructor at the courts in Central Park. His name is Jeremy, and he's maybe in his early thirties, slight, with glasses. He looks more like an English professor than a tennis pro. Sometimes we play sets—I can actually win a game now and then, gaining advantage from his powerful but uneven ground strokes. But mostly he talks. And talks. Jeremy has what he calls a Zen approach to tennis: it's not your strokes that count, it's what's in your head. He makes me come up and stand at the service line while he tosses balls at me. "Catch and release," he chants as I hit it gently back: "Catch and release." Encouraged by my progress, he deconstructs the exercise. "Do you see what's happening here? Your mind is giving up its attachment to the shot you just made. It's over. History. You're in the now. This shot."

Eventually he allows me to return to the baseline. As we rally, he's shouting directives. "Detach! Detach! Mindfulness is the key." I hit a few firm strokes, and at last we get something going. I'm hitting the ball on the sweet spot, getting in position, finding the Zone . . . when, suddenly, mid-rally, Jeremy reaches out and catches the ball. "See that?" he cries exultantly. "You're focused on the process. You're not trying to win. You're trying to find your inner rhythm."

I'm stunned. Rage courses through me. My best rally of the day, snuffed. Who is this guy, the Dalai Lama? But I'm afraid to complain: I don't want to seem unenlightened. It's not Jeremy's garrulity that's the problem, I tell myself: it's my resistance. Maybe he's right—I'm too invested in results, too attached to immediate rewards. Too Western.

After a lesson in which I'm allowed to swing at the ball maybe ten times during the whole hour, I finally crack. "There's so much discussion, Jeremy," I protest as we shake hands over the net. "I don't even break a sweat. At the end of a lesson I feel like I've been on the couch in a therapy session. I want to play tennis."

"That's the way I teach," he says firmly.

That was my last lesson with Jeremy.

I join a club across the river in Long Island City that has affordable rates and hire another instructor. He's from Jamaica, and his name is Wayne. The day I have my first lesson it's ninety-three degrees. Only three of the twelve courts are occupied: a pair of young men in crisp whites slamming the ball at each other and a foursome of elderly women in golf caps. Wayne gives me the standard evaluation, starting out on the service line and feeding me balls to determine my level.

My forehand is okay; it has some pace and goes in a fair percentage of the time. My backhand is another matter. I net ball after ball, often bouncing them into the net as if I were grounding out in a sandlot baseball game. When I try to adjust my swing, the ball loops into the alley. Wayne mimes the adjustments I need to make, his arm extended straight out to demonstrate that he's not breaking his wrist. The ball continues to land in the net or sail beyond the baseline. After a while he comes over to my side of the court, stands next to me, and shows me how to swing, clutching my arm to direct the trajectory. I have a sudden memory of Mike Fields, the tennis instructor at Birchwood Country

Club, holding my arm in just this way. It was 1956, the summer when I first took lessons. I add up the decades until I get to '96, then tack on seven years. I've been in pursuit of a better backhand for close to half a century.

Wayne retreats to his side of the court, pulls the wire basket of balls like a grocery cart to the service line, and begins feeding balls to my backhand. I continue to spray them long, wide, into the net. My frustration mounts, a compound of embarrassment and shame. I think of all the sports I've never mastered: squash, fly-fishing, pool. (Is pool a sport?) And all the other stuff, too: French, Italian, German, Czech, painting, poetry, fiction . . . Too late now.

Wayne is coming toward me, back across the court, wheeling the basket. I glance at my watch. I've been out here for fifty minutes: only ten minutes more. The heat is Saharan, the air sluggish and suffocating, the kind of weather guys drop dead in. I notice for the first time that there's no one else on the courts; the quartet of elderly women has dispersed; even the vigorous young men have retreated to a bench in the shade. I'm drenched in sweat and notice a stabbing, tightening sensation in my chest every time I swing at the ball.

Wayne positions himself on my side of the court, maybe twenty feet away. He reaches down, scoops a handful of yellow balls out of the basket, and begins to lob them at me. I hit a few over the net. "Move your feet," he instructs in his Caribbean lilt. My legs are trembling. I feel dizzy and clutch the chain-link fence, gazing at a green oasis of lawn on the other side like a convict yearning for freedom. But then, summoned out of God knows where, I get my second wind. Stumbling back and forth, I manage to hit five or six returns before Wayne throws one out of reach. I'm elated as I see the level of balls in the basket going down. Soon only a handful are left, then finally, none. It's a relief to trundle around the court pushing down on the pickup basket like a farmworker planting a row of corn.

"You're crazy," Anna comments when she finds me stretched out on the bed an hour later, curled up as if I've been kicked in the stomach. I raise my head from the pillow and say in a muffled voice: "I did it."

The college alumni magazine has arrived in the mail, and at midnight I'm still only at the class of '63—almost a decade short of my own class. I have yet to come across a single name I recognize, but it doesn't matter; reading Class Notes in chronological order affords the most concise summation of our progress toward decrepitude since Jaques's seven-ages-of-man speech in *As You Like It,* from "the infant mewling and puking in the nurse's arms" to "second childishness and mere oblivion, / Sans teeth, sans eyes, sans taste, sans everything."

I always begin at the beginning, with the nonagenarians and octogenarians: Bret is doing fine in the nursing home, "but his eyes continue to deteriorate." Dick, afflicted with "various arthritic complaints," has recently moved to an assisted-living facility with Edna, his wife of sixty-three years, now confined to a wheelchair with advanced Parkinson's. Joe is recovering from surgery for prostate cancer; Norman has senile dementia. Life's parameters are shrinking. "Too decrepit for the chores of country living, we've left our beloved lakeside cottage and moved to a condominium in town." The body is winding down, like a fan that's been unplugged and continues to rotate ever more slowly until it finally comes to a stop. Lew, at ninety-three, has finally been forced to give up golf. The Atkinsons haven't gone to Bermuda since Lucy broke her hip "When I look in the mirror I can hardly believe what I see," writes Phil. "I don't feel ninety."

The septuagenarians are more spry. Frank has had knee replacement but is back on the links; George is happy that he can still drive after an eye operation and revels in the "handicapped" parking sticker that gives him access to the best parking spots. The Warrens are still on the go "last year to Bologna, Nanjing, and the Maldives." Rogers is "as good as new" after a "double inguinal hernia repair job." Gordon loves to garden.

Working my way down to the sexagenarians, I'm impressed by their vigor (and let's hope sexagenarian means what it sounds like it should). The Morgans got in "two good weeks at Vail," the Logans hiked in the Alps, Everts "isn't even contemplating retirement" from his law firm. Their ranks, too, are thinning; some have cancer, some have died, but most are in the prime of life, going a mile a minute. "David travels so much that he's gotten lost at home finding his way to the bathroom in the middle of the night."

The guys in their fifties, my cohort, have "put feckless youth behind," in the words of a classmate, but there's hardly a word about bodily complaints; everyone's healthy, more or less. Reading glasses and trifocals have entered the picture, but boasts of heartiness predominate. Jones is learning to fly-fish, Skolnick still jogs three miles a day, "notwithstanding my rapidly receding hairline." Hopkins has joined the Polar Bear Club and broke the ice at a frozen lake in the Adirondacks. For this privileged crowd, or at least the self-selected subset that writes to alumni magazines, life is good.

It's even better for the classes a decade or so younger than mine—kids are being born (though parents are dying off). Physical prowess has been transferred to the young. The Haggertys' son is captain of the varsity baseball team. At ten, Sean "is turning out to be quite the speedy skater." "Besides sailing and soccer, my other main sport is one my five-year-old and I devised called Sofa Jumping." Others marvel that their infants are beginning to walk and talk.

The ones in their twenties, recent graduates, are too far upriver to hear the falls. They fly small airplanes and are serious about Ultimate Frisbee. They get married. They have no children. "We travel across the globe to climb volcanoes and make cheese." (Make cheese?) Physical activity plays a significant role in their lives. "Good hiking, running trails, swimming and boating . . ." The curtain is about to rise on the whole amazing story. "And so, from hour to hour, we ripe and ripe," says Jaques, "And then, from hour to hour, we rot and rot."

But not yet. One night I'm having a reunion with two classmates, Sam and Leonard, in Joe Allen's, a popular restaurant in the theater district. Actors drop in after curtain close and cluster at the bar. Sam has just sold a screenplay, and we're there to celebrate. He's been working on this screenplay for years, and whenever we saw each other he would say, "If I ever get this thing sold, let's go out and have a drunken dinner." So now it's been sold, and we're having the drunken dinner.

The waiter arrives and says, "Would any of you gentlemen like a cocktail?"

I'd like a vodka martini straight up, very dry, Grey Goose, with a twist.

"I'll have a Perrier and lime," I say to the waiter.

"Very good." He turns to Sam, awaiting his order.

"What kind of nonalcoholic beer do you have?"

"O'Doul's, I believe."

"Fine. I'll have an O'Doul's."

The waiter looks expectantly at Leonard.

Leonard: "Could I have a Coke?"

Welcome to the Designated Drivers Club.

Two years ago, I quit drinking. It wasn't as if I had an epiphany—I'm swearing off booze forever—or suffered a health scare, my internist palpating my liver and solemnly informing me I had incipient cirrhosis. It was just that my body couldn't take it any longer. I had less and less tolerance for alcohol. There had been a time when I could stay up late over dinner with friends, going through a bottle of wine apiece, then wake up the next morning and go to work with a clear head. In my early fifties I tapered off; two glasses of wine made me insomniac. I would wake up with a start in the middle of the night and listen to the grind of trucks down on Columbus Avenue, afraid of the next day's exhaustion. In the morning, I was groggy, tremulous, wired from too much coffee. In the bathroom mirror, I would glimpse a sallow, unhealthy face, the tallow-colored skin drawn tight.

But what was the alternative? Like any other aspiring writer, I was schooled in the literary trade's long tradition of drink. I knew the lore cold: Edmund Wilson used to chug down six martinis at a go. His journals are a chronicle of sodden days and nights: "Empty bottles of ginger ale and White Rock standing around the next morning—half-filled highball glasses, stale." "Drinking gin raw on the back porch." "Had all kinds of different colored things to drink." Alcohol was the fuel of genius. Malcolm Lowry drank himself to death in Mexico, F. Scott Fitzgerald drank himself to death in Hollywood, John Berryman drank himself to death in Minneapolis. Faulkner wandered the corridors of Random House drunk.

And it wasn't just writers who drank; the martini before dinner, the Bloody Mary at brunch, the highball in the club car on the way out to the suburbs after work—these were rituals inscribed in our parents' lives. Every home had a well-stocked liquor cabinet, the fifths of Smirnoff and Cutty Sark identified with pewter medals hung around their necks, and an array of paraphernalia: ice buckets, martini shakers, shot glasses, twizzle sticks, jars of green olives for martinis and maraschino cherries for Manhattans. When my parents had friends over, I'd stand at the top of the stairs in my pj's, the air down in the living room blue from cigarette smoke, and listen to the clink of glasses, the sharp crack of an ice tray being opened, as if trying to make out a secret code—the adult world, shrouded in mystery.

Those days are gone. At cocktail parties, I've noticed, the "full bar"—bourbon, scotch, vodka, gin, vermouth—is a rarity. Waiters circulate with trays bearing glasses of white wine and sparkling water. Drinking to excess is a social taboo. "I hear you shut down the Marriott bar," a colleague solemnly informed me the morning after I'd logged in a long night at the Modern Language Association convention. He might as well have said: "You were seen nodding off, a crack pipe at your feet, in a doorway at the Port Authority bus station."

As a Christmas present, a friend brings me a bottle of Famous Grouse. I pull the bottle from its coffin-shaped white box and cradle it in my hand, admiring the plump bird on the label, its small sharp beak and rainbow feathers. The amber liquid shines. I remember a story Gabriel García Márquez related in an interview: how when he decided to quit smoking, he took a pack of cigarettes out into the backyard of his house and buried it, sticking a little white cross on top. It was the funeral of his addiction, another loss to mourn—trivial in the scheme of things, a minor deprivation, but an addition to the ever-lengthening list of pleasures he would never in this life enjoy again.

Not only do we not drink or smoke; we don't eat either. At our drunken dinner, it's salads all around: Caesar; chicken; arugula (a kind of lettuce I'd never even heard of until a few years ago). No more cheeseburgers with bacon: I'd eat two bites and slump over the table like an outlaw shot dead in a bar fight.

The problem with this regimen is that I'm always starving. "A thin edge of hunger," my father used to counsel me. "That's the ticket to longevity." Fine, Dad, but as I recall, you yourself ate like a horse.

The waiter clears our table and prepares to take our coffee orders.

"A decaf espresso," I say. "Make that two," says Sam. Leonard orders a decaf cappuccino.

Whoopee.

At home, stripped down to my underpants for bed, I study myself in the full-length mirror. Not too bad. To be sure, some excess flesh spills over the waistband. And what about my thinning hair? Then there's the worsening curvature of the spine. As you get older, your cartilage hardens and the gaps between your bones shrink. You grow shorter, more compressed, like an accordion pressed inward. "Five feet, five and a half inches," my doctor calls out to the nurse who's transcribing data during my annual physical. "That can't be," I protest. "I used to be five-six. It says so on my driver's license." (I have an overwhelming temptation as I write this to up the whole exchange by an inch, but I'm trying to be honest.) "Five and a half inches," the doctor repeats firmly. Jesus Christ: so this is how the little old men you see shuffling down the street get to be that way. I hear my mother's long-ago admonition: stand up straight. For the next few days I walk around upright, my back rigid, like a bobby marching in front of Buckingham Palace.

The pills in my medicine cabinet tell a grisly tale. Lipitor to thin the blood, baby aspirin (one a day) to prevent blood clots, decongestant capsules the size of slugs to prevent me from snoring at night. Then there's the Minoxidil in a plastic canister that I empty over my pate each night, hopeful that it will grow hair the way it does in the TV ads ("Results guaranteed or your money back in thirty days"). I feel kind of ridiculous shaking the bottle upside down and pressing the two rubber dispensing teats against my scalp—the same motion I use to douse my half-portion of fries with ketchup. I also suffer from ailments for which there's no remedy: weakening vision; stiff joints; arthritic fingers. Can liver spots be far behind?

"Let's make a vow never to complain about our ailments," Anna says after an evening out with friends who dwelled in tedious detail on their bouts with irritable bowel syndrome, bleeding gums, arthritis, skin cancer, rheumatism, ringing in the ears. Someone claimed he had gout. Gout? I picture Dr. Johnson leaning on his cane, one leg stretched out on a chair.

"That's a good idea," I say, mindful of my eighty-seven-year-old mother, who tries so hard to be stoical but simply has to catalog her aches and pains; they are, after all, an increasingly central fact of her life. I'm intermittently aware of my body, conscious that it's beginning to break down. Mom is conscious of her body all the time. Nothing will relieve her dizziness; the doctors have tried everything. There is no cause. You might as well try to diagnose why a '57 Pontiac has trouble starting on a cold day.

"I've never felt better in my life," I write in to the alumni journal. "Still playing tennis, working out, getting whipped by my son. But I love the game as much as ever. In the last issue, Ned Brady wrote of having 'put feckless youth behind.' No argument there, but it could be worse. Had dinner with Sam Herbst and Leonard Janowitz not long ago: they both looked great."

I make it short. It's ten o'clock and time for bed.

1964

It's a blustery November afternoon, one of the last days of the tennis season. Dead leaves skitter across the court. We're the only ones out here. When I clutch the leather racket handle, my hand is so cold that I wish I had a golf glove. After six games, I'm still in my sweats; Dad has stripped down to his tennis whites. I admire his tough, stringy legs. He's still a tough old bird at fifty-one, but this could be my year. When I was fourteen, I vowed to beat him by the time I turned fifteen. I'm fifteen. It hasn't happened yet; all season he's held his own, fending off my determined assaults with a steely determination of his own. But we're even now at three apiece.

I play with confidence, rushing net and hitting even my second serve hard. After three deuces, I pull ahead 4–3, then break Dad's serve. Five-three.

He gives me a hard stare as he hands me a tennis ball at the net.

I can sense the impulse to lose begin to assert itself as I prepare to serve. If I beat him, will he not love me anymore?

I serve, rush net, and angle a volley well out of Dad's reach.

The next three points are hard-fought. Dad hugs the baseline, handling everything I throw at him. He's like a fierce trout on a line that won't give up. You reel and reel and can't bring him in. At thirty–all I serve an ace. Set point.

Forgive me, Dad. I know not what I do. Or rather, I do know, and do it anyway. I serve, heart pounding. Dad hits it back deep to my backhand. The shot is hard to handle, but I'm ready and decide to go for it. Bang! I slam it down the line.

Dad stands in the center of the court and watches the ball go by. The air is still. In the distance, I hear the hoot of the Northwestern train barreling toward Chicago.

We shake hands at the net.

Dad gives me a weak smile. He packs up his rackets and walks off the court toward the car in the empty parking lot.

Books

I'm packing up for our summer vacation, a week hiking out west. What books should I take? Every year it's a problem, and it's only getting worse. I always take too many, loading down my suitcase with their leaden weight. Books seem to grow longer every year; biographies— David McCullough's *John Adams*, Robert Caro's *Lyndon Johnson*— approach cinder block–like size. New novels, too, have reverted to the length (the width?) of the Victorian three-decker: Jonathan Franzen's *The Corrections*, Jeffrey Eugenides's *Middlesex*, Donna Tartt's *The Little Friend* announce their significance by their size. Big = important: the literary equation of our time. (Maybe it's *because* literature is no longer central to our time that it has to declare its significance in this way.) Or maybe it's literary inflation—too many books chasing too few readers.

I'm halfway through the Franzen—it's terrifically absorbing. The other two stare up at me reproachfully from my already overcrowded bedside table, the books piled up in a shaky ziggurat. No time! Already I'm bracing for the next round of incoming, praying they'll land on someone else's desk. Sleepless at dawn, I hear the *New York Times* land with a thump on the doorstep, so mammoth with its metastasizing sections—Circuits, Escapes, Dining Out—that I have to bend at the knees like a sumo wrestler to lift it off the doorstep. I'm even speed-reading the *New York Post*. On Monday the magazines arrive, wave after wave: *The New Yorker, New York Magazine, The New Republic*, and, every other week, *The New York Review of Books*. It's a commonplace to confess that you haven't read a book, just the reviews of it. Now even the reviews are more than I can manage. Skimming down the column of a Michiko Kakutani demolition job in the *Times*, I go straight to the last line: *lame, tired, a dud.* Never mind the trial, just give me the verdict, please: thumbs-up or -down. That's all I need to know. That's all I have time to know.

A friend shows up for lunch one day carrying a well-thumbed copy of *Invisible Man*. She's determined to catch up with classics she missed along the way: *Ulysses, Mrs. Dalloway, Lady Chatterley's Lover.* "I want to read these books while there's time." Skip the digressions, the subplots, the fine writing: she's in a hurry to get to the heart of the matter, the essence. "Do they end up together? Does she die in the end?"

The sense of urgency is so great that I take to listening to books on tape in the car. On long drives, we listen to Pepys's *Journals*, enthralled by his account of London burning, the plague, his adulterous escapades ("The girl refused nothing"). *The Iliad* is auditorially consumed as we go back and forth to Vermont. I feel guilty about imbibing books in this way, on the fly; the book is a sacred object, to be handled like a twelfth-century relic preserved in a moldering churchyard. To order up *The Great Courses: Teaching That Engages the Mind* off the Internet and pop a cassette in the dashboard seems like cutting corners. The civilized voice of Leo Damrosch, a Harvard professor of comparative literature, elucidates the development of the self in the Enlightenment while I whiz past Mobil stations, too enthralled even to stop for a CremeHorn and coffee.

Sometimes I think: why am I trying to cram more and more knowledge into my brain? It's getting a little late in the day. What good will it do to learn about Locke and Hobbes, Voltaire and Rousseau at this point? I've already read them once, in college, and can't remember a single thing about any of these guys except that Hobbes thought life was "nasty, brutish and short." So why go through the whole business again? But reading is like breathing—you don't stop until you're forced to stop for good. In his late eighties, my father was still attending Great Books classes, stuffing Plato and Dante into his forgetful head. On his bedside table in the intensive care unit during his last illness was a copy of *Ulysses.*

Not long ago I came across a troubling essay by Arthur Krystal, a recovering literary critic. Entitled "Closing the Books: A Devoted Reader Arrives at the End of the Story," Krystal's essay recounts in elegiac terms his disenchantment with the act of reading. "The sad truth is, I am unable to think seriously about any writer," he confesses. "Instead I think about what every middle-aged, nonliterary person thinks about: family, health insurance, money, property, time running out." The wisdom his favorite writers have imparted, the experiences they've worked through, are no longer news. "At some point we've all been down the same road."

I'm not quite as disillusioned as Krystal, but I share his impatience. I no longer have any compunction about putting down a book that doesn't tell me something I didn't already know. The novelist Nick Hornby writes a column in a hip new literary journal, *The Believer,* called "Stuff I've Been Reading," in which he provides a running account of his monthly progress through two categories: "Books Bought" and "Books Read." He's a very literary guy, and he reads a lot of books—I don't want to depict him as a slacker—but there was one column of his that really spoke to me. "Unfinished, abandoned, abandoned, unfinished," it begins. He, too, is having trouble in this area. "Boredom, and occasionally despair, is part of the reading life, after all."

Not the despair chronicled in books: the despair of ever having time to read them all, or even just a few. As that finite commodity grows shorter, a book has less and less time to make the cut. Like an actor trying out for a part, it's got to grab me right away or it's "Thank you, Mr. X, we'll be in touch."

What happened? Why don't we read the way we did, consumed, obsessed, oblivious to the world around us? My own sense is that developments in technology have fatally interfered with the cultivation of basic literacy. The hurried pace of life erodes our capacity to read. The blizzard of new, ingenious, and largely pointless technology that saturates the airwaves and our brain waves in the form of cell phones and faxes—amazing when invented, already obsolete, superseded by e-mail and the insidious BlackBerry, which enables you to read your e-mail while loitering on a park bench—makes a tough job even tougher. Much as I savor the experience of immersion in a good book, the way it takes over your life, *becomes* your life, my Samsung gleams at my side, speed-dial at the ready. Stretched out on an August afternoon, fighting my way through the first chapter of *The Possessed* for the tenth time, I feel tense and coiled, waiting for a call from my agent.

So where can you read these days? Planes are ideal. (Even there it's possible to hook up your laptop and send e-mail or make calls from those phones embedded in the seats.) After intense deliberation, I've chosen the Faber edition of Wordsworth's *Selected Poems;* a dysfunctional-family memoir that got a great review in the *Times;* and—my favorite book of all time—Boswell's biography of Samuel Johnson.

And yet . . . after watching the in-flight movie and *Everybody Loves Raymond,* I spy a tattered copy of the American Airlines magazine tucked into the pocket of the seat in front of me. Let's see: here's an interesting article about what's doing in Seattle, and "The Best Steakhouses in Dallas"—a must-read, though I've never been to Dallas and have no intention of ever going there. Why do I read *The American Way*? As Sir Edmund Hillary said when asked why he climbed Mount Everest: because it's there.

By the time I open my *Boswell,* the stewardess—I mean the flight attendant—is directing us to stow our tray tables and return our seats to the upright position.

I'm more independent than I used to be. "To feel for ourselves the greatness of a book, we may have to risk that we may not like it," confessed Alain de Botton on the *Times*'s op-ed page. "We have to make our own minds up, which requires us to be somewhat irreverent, and dare to think that perhaps Jane Austen is a drag, Charles Dickens melodramatic and Virginia Woolf prissy. Perhaps they're not, but we'll never know for ourselves, in our own hearts, until we develop the inner security to judge for ourselves." De Botton is in excellent company. John Berryman, one of our most distinguished poets and the author of a highly regarded collection of essays on Shakespeare, admitted in a *Dream Song:* "Literature bores me, especially great literature." Philip Larkin wrote: "Books are a load of crap." They weren't to be taken literally; they were rebelling against a long-buried, long-suppressed urge to defy the authority of what has come to be known as "the canon"—the classics of Western civilization. Who says Tennyson is great? Why should I slog through Pope's *Dunciad*?

For a long time I made it a point of pride never to admit I hadn't read a book, no matter how obscure. If someone mentioned Leibniz's *Discourse on Metaphysics* or Arnold Bennett's deservedly forgotten miscellany, *Things That Have Interested Me,* I would mutter, "Oh, yes, I know it." And I invariably did, having come across a reference to it in some other book or even having purchased a copy with the intent of "getting around to it." Lately, though, I've discovered that I can admit ignorance with greater ease.

I no longer care about keeping up, or even the pretense of keeping up. I have no syllabus. I'm thirty-plus years out of college and mercifully beyond the reach of my college tutor, Sim Wade, a courtly southern gentleman who once broke off a tutorial with me upon hearing that I hadn't finished *Middlemarch*. "Your loss," he had said tersely, ushering me out the door. I'm sorry, Sim (wherever you are); the truth is, I still haven't finished it, and probably never will. But I'm sure he's right: it *is* a loss, and so I've fetched my copy down from the shelf. It's right there on the coffee table, its pages brittle with age; I pass it every day, glancing at the cover, a nineteenth-century portrait of George Eliot in a pastoral landscape, gazing over a fence. Her back is turned, as if in reproach. *You have turned your back on me, so I shall turn my back on you.* Sometimes, seized with guilt and yearning, I pick it up and hold it in my hand, as if it were an artifact rather than a book. I admire its heft—what would it be like to lead a life in which this book could be read through? I speed-read the introduction by W. J. Harvey, professor of English at the Queen's University of Belfast, "who died in 1967" (the year I bought the book). "Before we consider the social unity of *Middlemarch* . . ." Something, alas, that I'll never have time to do. I longingly scan the notes at the end, so rich in erudition. "(p. 219). *The most brilliant English critic:* A reference to Hazlitt's *Notes of a Journey through France and Italy* (1826). (I owe this reference to Mrs. E.E. Duncan-Jones)." What a terrific name. Who is she? Or, more likely at this point, who *was* she? I imagine Mrs. E.E. Duncan-Jones in her cozy, book-filled cottage in the Cotswolds, or perhaps her grand estate with a library, the top shelves reachable only by a ladder attached to an iron rail, drowsing over a leather-bound volume of Hazlitt, a cup of tea by her side. And now here I am at the last page—not of the text, but of the physical object—greedily eyeing a list of "Some Recent Volumes" (not anymore): *Waverly,* by Sir Walter Scott; *Northanger Abbey,* by Jane Austen; *The Old Curiosity*

Shop, by Charles Dickens. Do I know these books? Obviously. Have I read them? Not a one. Let it go.

That I have no time to read books doesn't stop me from buying them. I order books from Amazon; I buy them from vendors on the street, enjoying the ritual: the coveted volume cradled in the hand, the purchase mulled, the commitment made, the money extracted from the wallet, the surge of pride as one closes the deal. *I read, therefore I am.* The instant I walk through the door of Barnes & Noble I'm in trouble. There, on the front table, are the "new releases," a good 60 or 70 percent of which I long to read. Peter Ackroyd's thick *London: A Biography;* Donald Kagan's *The Peloponnesian Wars,* Frank M. Turner's massive biography of John Henry Newman, a new translation of Dante (if I buy it, I'll own three, all unread). I'm seized with a feeling of desperation that intensifies as I penetrate the further reaches of the store: my eye flits over John Julius Norwich's *Venice,* Chesterton's *Saint Francis of Assisi,* Noel Annan's *The Dons: Mentors, Eccentrics and Geniuses.* In the end, I buy a fat Penguin paperback collection of Kierkegaard's writings and return home to read four pages of his journals before consigning it to the tottering pile.

And what about the books I long to reread—absurd thought, given the press of more books, freshly acquired and adored? Looking up from my desk, I glimpse *The Letters of Virginia Woolf,* Dr. Johnson's *Lives of the Poets,* A. J. A. Symons's *The Quest for Corvo:* books I once loved but forgot I own. I vow (so many vows) to organize them all; I have so many books that I can't keep track of them. Several times I've bought a second copy of a book that I couldn't find on my haphazard shelves even though I know it's there.

Once a month, a catalog called *The Common Reader* arrives in the mail. Lovingly produced by a mail-order house in a New York City suburb, it features over a hundred pages of books. The sole criterion for inclusion is the endorsement of the company's founder, James Mustich, a fanatical bibliophile. Each catalog is prefaced by a brief letter. In one, he quotes Emerson: " 'Tis the good reader that makes the good book, for the profoundest thought or passion sleeps as in a mine, until it is discovered by an equal mind and heart." Mustich is a good reader, and puts me to (further) shame. He organizes his selections into eccentric categories of his own devising—"Boundaries & Borders," "History's Mysteries," "Destinations," "Memory Speaks"—and appends his own brief commentaries. Who could resist *The Long Walk,* by Slavomir Rawicz, an account of the author's escape from a Soviet labor camp in Siberia in the company of six prisoners who "had no map and no compass, only an ax head, a homemade knife, and a fierce determination to survive." *The Long Walk,* claims Mustich, "remains among the most heroic, compelling stories I've ever read." (Likewise for me, only substitute "never" for "ever.") Who could resist this recommendation of William Gibson's *A Mass for the Dead*? "It is a work whose rendering of experience so eloquently shaped what I knew, or intuited, about existence that my sense of self, family, and world would be unrecognizable to me without it."

Sold! Unable to resist, I add *Biblioholism: The Literary Addiction,* by one Tom Raabe, and fill out the invoice, $73.29 the poorer in cash but soon to be the richer in wisdom (even if I only get to page thirty of one of my new acquisitions and never so much as crack the others). A month later, when the new issue of *The Common Reader* arrives, I order Shelby Foote's magnificent three (three!)-volume history of the Civil War in a boxed set. Why do I say *magnificent*? Because the first chapter of the first book is so vivid, so engrossing, so rich in detail, that I can't put it down—until I do, never to pick it up again because a new packet of books has arrived in the mail. When I contemplate Foote's tripledecker in its box atop the piano, I can hardly wait to get old. A friend of mine tells me that her father read through Dickens on his deathbed.

Like the drinker who treats his hangover with "the hair of the dog," I assuage my anxiety about all the books I've bought and not read by purchasing more. Somehow I imagine that if I buy a book I'll read it. Time will stop; the day will mysteriously expand its number of hours. Suetonius's *Lives of the Poets* will be absorbed by osmosis; Ben Franklin's *Autobiography,* a slender volume, will—if it sits on the coffee table long enough—*feel* as if I've read it. Here's a book I need, or think I need: Giannozzo Manetti's *Biographical Writings.* When it arrives in the mail, ordered from an advertisement in *The New York Review of Books,* I open the package and discover that the left-hand page is in Latin—which suddenly, to my advantage now, I never learned to read. Which means it's only *half as long as I thought it was.* Yes! A distinct possibility that it will get read, that one. Yet, to my sorrow, it doesn't. It survives cut after cut, as my books, like the hapless hitters in spring training, get shipped off to the farm team: the Strand down on Fourth Avenue, which buys secondhand books. Every few months, a genial guy with a ponytail arrives with folded boxes, knocks them open, and trundles down the hall with his loaded cart, disappearing into the freight elevator. So long, fellows. Sorry it didn't work out.

Childhood was the Golden Age of Reading. At ten, I would check out the works of John R. Tunis or Walter R. Brooks's *Freddy the Pig* series under the vigilant direction of Miss Boyé, the children's librarian of our public library, and bicycle home with a bulging knapsack of books strapped to my back, so top-heavy that it made my Schwinn teeter.

I loved the total absorption in a private world, a world sealed off from the so-called real world, in which people got sick and lost jobs, parents fought at the dinner table, bills had to be paid. Seated cross-legged on the floor, head bowed as if in prayer, I was beyond distraction:

sirens, doorbells, calls to supper went unheeded and unheard. It was as if life itself was merely a medium, like air, that enabled literature to thrive. "I can always tell when you're reading somewhere in the house," Francis Spufford recalls his mother saying in his charming bildungsroman of bibliophilia, *The Child That Books Built: A Life in Reading:* "There's a special silence, a *reading* silence."

My favorite genre was the coming-of-age classic: Maugham's *Of Human Bondage*, Ring Lardner Jr.'s *The Ecstasy of Owen Muir*, Goethe's *The Sorrows of Young Werther.* The salvation of their tortured protagonists lay in escape—a theme that had intense resonance for me when I was seventeen. Much as I enjoyed the perks of my soft suburban life—cars in the garage, private tennis lessons at the club—I longed to inhabit some other, more exalted world. Up in my room, I communed with Stendhal's Fabrice del Dongo, the doomed boy in *The Charterhouse of Parma* who never quite finds his footing in the swirl of European history; Flaubert's Fréderic Moreau, another "outsider" wandering through the great events of his time in a haze; and Joyce's melancholy Stephen Dedalus, determined "to forge in the smithy of [his] soul the uncreated conscience of [his] race."

In college, my book fever continued unabated. Night after night I sat at a long table in the library and fought my way through Aquinas, Hegel, Hume, Locke, Mill. I read Carlyle's *History of the French Revolution* and Trevelyan's *History of England.* Three decades later, I come across my Anchor paperback of Trevelyan, jaundice-colored now, the pages flaking and brittle. Key passages have been underscored with a yellow Magic Marker: "Feudalism is the characteristic institution of the Middle Ages; it implies a fixed and legal subordination of certain classes of society to certain others, to obtain civilized order at the expense of barbaric anarchy." It's hard to believe that I once knew this stuff cold.

English literature was my concentration—a good word to describe the stubborn dedication with which I read in those years. Our primary textbook was the *Norton Anthology of English Literature,* two massive paperbacks with tissue-thin, nearly transparent pages. Hunched over my desk late at night, the light from a goosenecked lamp trained on the tiny-lettered texts, I made my single-minded way through the corpus, straining to decipher the odd dialects that metamorphosed, after a two-thousand-page trek, into *The Waste Land.* We began with the archaic, singsong *Beowulf,* then galloped through bawdy Chaucer, Spenser's *Faerie Queene,* the Elizabethans, the Jacobean playwrights and the metaphysical poets, Sir Thomas Browne's creepy *Urne-Burial,* the stately Augustan verse of Dryden and Pope, the florid romantics, the boring Victorians, and finally, panting toward the finish line as spring crocuses bloomed under the open lecture-hall windows, the beloved moderns, Yeats and Eliot. What thrilled me about this chronology was that it told a story, one voice building upon another. Tradition, wrote Eliot, "cannot be inherited, and if you want it you must obtain it by great labor." Great labor: the poet had it right.

I liked "working up" a subject—going to the library or the bookstore and staggering home with an armful of books by a single author, learning my way around an unfamiliar style and sensibility, a point of view, a voice; reading up on the period; studying, elbows planted with wonky determination on my desk, the "secondary literature" (critics, biographers, historians); and, after a few days or weeks, finally beginning to feel sure-footed on this once-uncharted terrain. Inspired by the impulse purchase of Quentin Bell's little book on Ruskin in a second-hand shop on the Charing Cross Road, I would discover that it was imperative to acquaint myself with *The Stones of Venice;* and then, having picked up somewhere along the way a decrepit edition of that work, to realize that I simply must read the author's secretive but revealing autobiography, *Praeterita,* which led me back to George Painter's chap-

ter on Ruskin in his biography of Proust . . . and so on, until at last
released by the epiphany, prompted by a glimpse of Macaulay's *History
of England* on a display table in Blackwell's, that I had to know what the
Restoration exactly *was*—upon which my preoccupation with Ruskin
was usurped by a pressing need to get a handle on English history.

I was especially drawn to Penguin Books. You could recognize them
across a room by their spines: black for nineteenth-century European
novels (Flaubert, Goethe, Tolstoy, Turgenev); blue for modern history
and culture (Ernest Jones's life of Freud; Ernst Fischer's *The Necessity of
Art*); orange for nineteenth-century English fiction (Dickens, Trollope,
George Eliot); and gray for modern English fiction (Conrad, Henry
James, Ford Madox Ford). Balzac was an addiction. Penguin had given
his books curious titles in translation—*History of the Thirteen*, *The
Chouans*, *A Harlot High and Low*. I was shocked (and titillated) by *The
Wild Asses' Skin*, with its parade of gamblers, lowlifes, whores, and
"voluptuaries"—what an evocative word!—sunk in debauchery, and its
astonishingly vivid orgy scene, at the height of which "groups of
entwined figures mingled confusedly with the noble masterpieces of
white marble sculpture adorning the suites of rooms." I must have read
twenty-odd of the hundred-and-some novels Balzac wrote in his caf-
feinated mania.

Thirty-five years later, I can scarcely remember a single plot. (Plot is
the first thing to go: I couldn't even remember the plot of *Persuasion*
until I saw it one night on *Masterpiece Theatre*.) One book, however, has
stayed with me: *Lost Illusions*. The spine of my copy is creased with
white lines, evidence of hard reading. I was mesmerized by the story of
the poet Lucien Chardon's journey from a provincial village to the haut
monde of Paris and his descent into hack journalism—which didn't
seem like such a precipitous descent to me. (Wasn't a journalist still a
writer?) A clueless midwestern aspirant to the great world, I needed

information: How did social class work? What was the role of money in the determination of status? How did you embark on a career? I was like the young man Balzac describes "who has no idea where he is making for, wonders where the Palais-Royal is when he is standing in front of it and asks a passerby the way to the Louvre only to be told 'You're looking at it.'"

Anna Karenina, too, I can sort of remember—even where I first read it. When Kitty gives birth, I was standing in the aisle of a crowded London tube, holding the fat paperback open with one hand and gripping a strap with the other. Levin waits for hours, nervously pacing and fretting, bustling in and out of Kitty's room; and, as the moment arrives, his wife shrieking in the pain of childbirth, the doctor frowning, the midwife somber, he's convinced that Kitty is about to die. Suddenly it's over, the baby is in the midwife's arms, and Levin's adored wife is gazing at him with peaceful, loving eyes: "The taut strings snapped, and the sobs and tears of joy which he had never foreseen rose within him with such force that they shook his whole body." There, in the swaying train, the green fields falling away like a parted sea outside the smudged window, I wept alongside Levin in a fit of rhapsodic grief. Why? I don't have a clue. I was twenty-three, nowhere near the births of my own children. Reading that passage at fifty-four, I'm still moved by the scene; I know exactly what Levin feels when he marvels over the mystery of creating a life—"another human being who had not existed a moment ago but who, with the same rights and importance to itself as the rest of humanity, would live and create others in its own image."

But the scene that has the most shattering effect on me now is the one where Levin's half-brother, Koznyshev, goes out walking in the woods to pick mushrooms with Kitty's friend Varenka. They're clearly on the verge of falling in love; Koznyshev, middle-aged and still a bachelor, has made up his mind to propose. ("He remembered Varenka's saying that it was only in Russia that men regarded themselves as old at fifty, and that in France a man of fifty considers himself *dans la force de l'age*.") But as they loiter in the forest, each prepared for Koznyshev's momentous declaration, some inexplicable impulse prompts Varenka to break the silence with a pointless remark about mushrooms. Koznyshev replies with a fungus-related observation of his own. ("What is the difference between a white boletus and a birch mushroom?") The spell is broken. The moment has passed. "What was to have been said would not be said."

Why does this scene so affect me now? It dramatizes with unbearable poignance an experience that can only be understood when you're of a certain age—and that is the experience of finality, of choices made that cannot be undone. Tolstoy was nearly fifty when he wrote this scene and had known deep sorrow and regret. The death of his mother when he was only two, and of his father eight years later; a troubled adolescence that led to a halfhearted suicide attempt; repeatedly flunking out of college; the pileup of debts from gambling in the army; religious crises of doubt and faith; his brother's death from tuberculosis (an event that would be described with harrowing vividness in *Anna Karenina*): this was Tolstoy's life. The failure of Koznyshev and Varenka to consummate their liaison was a haunting portrait of missed chances. What could have happened would not happen.

One of the most cherished legacies of the reading life is that you can pass it on to your children. You've *got* to read *Crime and Punishment*. You've *got* to read *Tender Is the Night*. The only book in my adolescent pantheon that my daughter rejected was *Look Homeward, Angel*. "It's no good," she said curtly. "I guess you read it too late," I replied, eager to defend a book I'd devoured as a highbrow kid. "If I'd read it when I was twelve, it still would have been no good," she shot back. Her private-school education had made her too sophisticated for Thomas Wolfe; how could you expect a child who's reading Ovid in the original to appreciate Wolfe's incantatory raving?

Intrigued by her disdain, I fetched my old Scribner's edition down from the shelf and leafed through it until I came to a passage that stopped me: "Thus, pent in his dark soul, Eugene sat brooding on a fire-lit book, a stranger in a noisy inn. The gates of his life were closing him in from their knowledge, a vast aerial world of phantasy was erecting its fuming and insubstantial fabric. He steeped his soul in streaming imagery." This was an account of the books Eugene Gant read as a boy, his discovery of the power of literature. Over the top in the age of postmodernist irony, no doubt; but when I came to the scene where Eugene's brother Ben dies of tuberculosis, his entire family gathered around him in witness—"They grew quiet and calm, they plunged below all the splintered wreckage of their lives, they drew together in a superb communion of love and valiance, beyond horror and confusion, beyond death"—I sat stunned on Molly's bed for a long time. My sensibility, hardened by the defiant anti-pathos of Mailer and Roth, had built up a resistance to the sentimental; Wolfe's florid, hyperventilating prose broke it down, invading the hardy immune system of adult critical discrimination and demonstrating just how susceptible it still is to the storms of adolescent excess.

When William was assigned to read *The Catcher in the Rye* for ninth-grade English class, I decided again to refresh my memory so we could have one of those talks you're supposed to have at the dinner table. The thing is, as Holden Caulfield might have put it, I already *knew* just about everything that was in the goddam book. It was all in my head: the scene with the whore in the hotel; the conversation with this cabdriver Horwitz about what happens to the ducks in the Central Park lagoon in winter ("I mean does somebody come around in a truck or something and take them away?"); that scene at the end where he buys a ticket for Phoebe to ride the carousel in Central Park and it starts to rain but he just sits on the bench and waves to her as she goes around and around in her blue coat.

"What's sad is the way he keeps getting betrayed," I say to Will. "He can't trust anyone except his sister."

"That's not true," Will says. "Look at Mr. Antolini"— the old teacher Holden goes to see.

"Mr. Antolini comes on to him," I remind him.

"What are you talking about?"

"Mr. Antolini comes over to Holden on the couch and starts patting him on the head in the dark while he's asleep," I explain, ever the patient critic. "What do you think he's doing?"

William will have none of it. He insists that Mr. Antolini is just being nice. Later that night I go look up the scene. You could read it either way: the teacher, oiled up by highballs—I like that old word — begins to lose his inhibitions; or Mr. Antolini is gazing at his student with innocent affection ("I'm simply sitting here, admiring—"), touched by Holden's loneliness . . . Is this ambiguity a vindication of the unstable narrator that preoccupied us during the era when deconstruction ruled college English departments? To me, Mr. Antolini is a figure of pathos, sensitive, unfulfilled, a middle-aged man whose conflicted sexuality requires the salve of alcohol. To my fifteen-year-old son, he's a kindly teacher being generous toward a screwed-up former student. We sit at the dinner table and discuss. Suddenly I think of Mr. Reque, my high school English teacher, talking in class about the book. You know that scene where Holden says that when you read a great book you want to call up the author? I want to call up Mr. Reque. I wonder if he's listed—if he's alive. He wouldn't be that old, maybe in his late sixties or early seventies. That's the strange thing about the teachers you had in high school: they weren't that much older than you, so a lot of them would still be around. I get up from the table and call information: I still remember the Chicago area code. Oh God: he's listed. If I push the number one, they'll connect me to Mr. Reque *right now.* I'm tempted: I want to ask him what he thinks of Mr. Antolini. But I come to my senses and hang up the phone.

God

Standing beside me, my friend Lenny is reciting the Neilah in Hebrew—the "concluding service," it says at the bottom of the page of my Yom Kippur prayer book—muttering as he rocks back and forth on the balls of his feet like a sailor on a sea-battered ship.

At fifty-three, I'm attending my third service, a guest at Lenny's congregation. It all started when I happened upon a flyer taped to the door of the Lincoln Square Synagogue as I was walking by: "At last, the High Holiday Service for those who aren't so High on the Holidays." I read on:

Not looking forward to Rosh Hashanah and Yom Kippur again this year?

Feel like you go to synagogue out of guilt and feel even more guilty after you leave?

Don't understand the language or the rituals?

Seems the rabbi is talking to everyone but you?

Like one of those tests they have in *Reader's Digest* that you read at the dentist's office—"Find out if you're an alcoholic . . . happily married . . . bipolar . . ."—the four questions (why did that phrase sound familiar?) were impossible to ignore. I ran down the list and answered all four in the affirmative. The results proved incontrovertible: I was a deracinated, nonobservant Jew. And a very extreme case, as it happened. The rabbi wasn't talking to me because I was never in a place where I might be listening to the rabbi; I hadn't been to services in over forty years, and even then it was only because my parents wanted to hear the famous baritone Richard Tucker at the Medinah Temple in Chicago.

This state of extreme agnosticism had never troubled me. I was satisfied to drift through the world indifferent to a question—or was it a condition? a state of mind? a philosophical or perhaps ontological issue?—that had preoccupied the vast majority of mankind throughout all of recorded history: the existence of God. What, it might be asked, did I think *Paradise Lost, The Brothers Karamazov,* the poems of Hopkins and Donne, and a thousand other works of literature that I'd encountered in the course of two decades of schooling and three more decades of erratic but compulsive reading were in fact *about*? I had read even the Bible as a book, not as a text that had ministered to humanity's hopes and wishes—prayers, they were called—had offered consolation, insight, inspiration to billions of souls. I had been vaguely aware that it was the source of numerous stories that were common lore: Job had a very hard time, Jonah was swallowed by a whale, Moses heard the Ten Commandments. I had noticed that when I opened the top drawer of desks and bureaus in hotels, *Why, there it was,* bound in austere black leather.

My ignorance of Judaism was matched only by my ignorance of Christianity—Christmas in my childhood was for gift giving and decorating the tree. (Didn't every Jew have one?) We had a menorah, too, made of brass by my bachelor uncle Benny in his basement workshop in my grandparents' home—I liked to light the candles, adding one a night. But I preferred to watch the program of carols televised live from the King's College Chapel in Cambridge, England, on Christmas Day. *Unto Us a Son Is Born:* and who might that be? I secularized what many considered the greatest achievements of Western civilization, experiencing them as works of art. The iconography of Jesus hung from the walls of every museum I'd ever visited. What did I make of Giotto and Bernini, Raphael and Tintoretto? What exactly did I imagine was being depicted in those works, in the plump cherubim and saints with saucerlike halos? What of the churches themselves, those soaring edifices in whose gloomy, pigeon-infested interiors my family huddled with our guidebooks on my first trip to Europe? I had been in Saint Peter's Square with my parents when the Pope himself, a distant white-robed figure, appeared on the balcony of his quarters and prayed before an adoring throng. Why all the commotion?

The people I saw muttering in their pews on those rare occasions when I stumbled into a church seemed vaguely pathetic to me. Poor deluded souls. Whom did they suppose they were addressing? Who would hear their prayers? Religion, to a child of the 1960s who considered himself a Marxist, is the opium of the masses; and, as for the vexing question of how the universe came into being, that was a matter for physicists to resolve. My eyes were resolutely focused on this world. The rest was illusion; belief was designed to pacify those unprepared to accept its essential meaninglessness. My theologians remained my earliest intellectual heroes: T. S. Eliot, Beckett, Joyce. "There's your God," says Stephen Dedalus to his teacher, Mr. Deasy, in the midst of a heated argument about faith: "A shout in the street."

My disregard for religion was unsurprising, given the determinedly secular environment in which I was raised. My parents, like many second-generation Jews, had no patience with organized religion, which seemed to them synonymous with the shtetl; the very idea of observing the High Holidays would have seemed as retrograde to them as wearing broad-brimmed black hats and *pais.*

That there was a class element to this haste to leave behind their origins only occurred to me much later. Atheism, in my parents' scheme of things, was assimilationist, the road to becoming American. What they didn't realize was that religious belief—or anyway, worship—could also be a way *up* in society. Even among Jews, there were exclusive congregations—my parents could never have gotten into Temple Emanu-El, the domed Gold Coast synagogue that cost half a million dollars to join. Religion, like everything in America—like everything in world history—was class-striated. German Jews looked down on Russian Jews; Lithuanian Jews looked down on Ukrainian Jews. On the home front, the Lakeshore Country Club trumped our club, Birchwood, six tennis courts and a swimming pool with a cinder-block clubhouse, out by Edens Highway. But a Jew was a Jew. Money might enable you to move up in class *as a Jew;* it wouldn't necessarily make you more American.

I suppose my parents, obeying the dialectic that ordained each generation should do the opposite of the previous generation, could at least have gone, like most of their friends, to Congregation Israel, the Reform synagogue on the North Shore presided over by the popular and erudite Rabbi Wolf, who sprinkled his sermons with references to Spinoza and Simone Weil; but they were so stubbornly against worship in any form that even the postmodernist edifice that housed that insanely affluent congregation was equated in their minds with a dank Odessa shul. They saw no reason for me to be bar mitzvahed. As far as they were concerned, I would become a man in good time whether I could recite passages from the Torah or not. Besides, the religious component in the suburban bar mitzvah was minimal. My friends, on their thirteenth birthdays, were called to manhood with lavish parties at the Standard Club, replete with limousines and circus acts and brand-name bands, in order to display their families' wealth. It wasn't spiritual growth that counted; it was compound growth.

Thus it was—as they say in the old stories—that I had gotten far beyond the midpoint of my life without ever having addressed, or even been more than dimly aware of, the one experience common to all peoples and civilizations on the planet. On rare occasions I had the faintest glimmer of a recognition that the unexplained mystery of how this came to pass (and what was *this*? The stars in the heavens? The billions of souls on the planet? The splendor of the natural world?) might constitute a worthy subject of meditation. One I recall in particular. It was November in London and I was on a journalistic assignment, writing a profile of the famous biographer Richard Holmes, I was on a high, having worked hard for a week and harvested the material for my story. I would be flying home in the morning. It was early evening, and as I walked through Trafalgar Square on the way back to my hotel, I passed the Church of St. Martin-in-the-Fields. A sign on the door announced a concert that was just then about to begin. On a whim, I bought a ticket. The church was nearly full. The seats on the main floor were all occupied, so I climbed the stairs to the balcony and sat down in one of the hard pews. For the next hour, the music of Mozart's horn concertos filled the air, a dizzying cascade of sound. When I came out, it had started to drizzle, and the streets shimmered like rivers, bearing along on their burnished surface a flood of black taxis. Maybe I was just overstimulated, but the experience—the music, the candles flickering on the altar, the blur of headlights in the rain—seemed incomplete; I couldn't process it and let it go. For weeks afterward, the memory of that night in

London haunted me. Whenever I thought of it, I was gripped with a sudden exalted joy. But I was also confused. How could a scene of such intense and vivid beauty turn out to be so transient? How could it—and everything—simply vanish from the earth? I dismissed my bafflement as an excess of mental data.

In New York, the High Holidays produced in me a sensation of melancholy. I could never figure out whether to stay home from work or go and face the empty desks in my office. The streets were deserted; New York is a Jewish city. I got depressed seeing the families strolling in their holiday finery, the women with their flowery hats, the men and boys in dark suits and shiny shoes. They didn't seem hurried or bent upon some daily errand, the way people usually did in the city; they seemed happy and serene, buoyed up by their morning in synagogue. I envied them.

A few days after my encounter with the flyer from the Lincoln Square Synagogue, I put on my black suit, reserved until then for business meetings and grandparents' funerals, and walked down 77th Street to the Historical Society in the fading autumn light. For some reason—no raw recruits in synagogue?—services were being held off-site. Entering the auditorium where I had gone on other days to watch the occasional documentary about the Civil War or Dutch settlers in New York, I was mildly alarmed at the emptiness of the rows and rows of plush velvet seats. Scattered about at a vast distance from one another, huddled in their solitude, were three or four solitary souls, hunched over black prayer books. I took a snowy tallith from a table and a jet-black yarmulke from a bowl and found a seat equidistant from the others. Would even a minyan—I had picked up the term from Irving Howe's *World of Our Fathers*—show? Eventually nine or ten new recruits trickled in, and a pair of robed rabbis materialized from behind the curtain onstage like a vaudeville team. One was tall and one was short. The tall one was from Lincoln Square, no doubt cursing under his breath the assignment that had landed him before this dolorous congregation on the High Holidays; his colleague, he explained, had come all the way from Israel on a pilgrimage to round up wayward Jews. For the next hour, following the quavery sounding of the shofar, they walked us through the service, performing what I can only describe as a shtick. " 'Why is this night different from all other nights?' Oops! Wrong service," joked Short. "Rosh Hashanah," explained Tall, addressing us as if we were gentiles on a field trip, "celebrates the Jewish New Year. It symbolizes Moses' descent from the mountain with the Second Tablets, inscribed with the testament of God's forgiveness and love. That's why we celebrate this day." In between borscht belt jokes ("Three Jews are walking down a street in Brooklyn . . ."), they guided us through the service, alternately chanting in Hebrew, reading in English, and explaining the text as they went along. At odd moments—their import was never explained—the rabbis and a young cantor, who had been introduced to us as a student at Juilliard, broke into song.

To my surprise, I began to feel at ease—sort of. I liked the language of the service, the invocation to an ancient people to look inward and seek redemption from the Creator, the blessings "which You lavish upon us in forest and sea, in mountain and meadow, in rain and sun." I was moved by the address, at once intimate and shy, to Eternal God, "Who spread forth the heavens and established the earth, and whose glorious presence can be found everywhere." But I was annoyed by the rabbis' overly familiar manner. They kidded around, offered up parables as if they were *Seinfeld* skits, and apologized whenever they lapsed into Hebrew: "You're not gonna understand this next part . . ." At one point—and this was the deal breaker for me—they interrupted the service and asked the congregation, which had by this time broken through to double figures, to introduce ourselves to our neighbors. I might as well have been at an AA meeting: *Hi, my name is Jim and I'm a Jew* . . . We were then invited to go around the room and say a few words about ourselves and why we had come. There was a Japanese exchange student; a middle-aged couple who had both been raised in unobservant homes and had shown up out of the same inchoate impulse that had brought me there; a young Catholic woman from Ecuador who was visiting her sister who worked for an office-cleaning firm in Midtown; an elderly man who lived down the block and didn't feel up to walking the nine blocks to Lincoln Square ("I have a little indigestion"); and a dozing homeless person in a raincoat who couldn't be roused to share his biography.

I was disheartened by the atmosphere—the sparseness and randomness of the congregation, the secular venue, the jocular tone of the rabbis. But my hunger for connection was so insistent that I persuaded myself to tolerate the provisional nature of the service. A phrase of Coleridge came to mind: poetry required "the willing suspension of disbelief." (My knowledge of English literature was by this time vestigial, but every once in a while a scrap of quotation surfaced.) Before long, I was chanting the Yigdal in transliterated Hebrew at the top of my lungs (*Yigdal Elohim hai v'yish-tabah, / Nimtza v'eyn yet el m'tzi-uto*) as if I'd grown up trotting off to Sunday school with a prayer book in my satchel. The tall rabbi told us the story of God's covenant with the Jews and how on this holiday we celebrated God's dominion over all and looked inward with a self-critical eye, judging, atoning, resolving—but in the end, as I understood it, giving ourselves a pass. The King of Kings both accepted our flaws and invited us to change. Fair enough. Our ragged congregation spoke as one: "In the book of life and blessing, peace and prosperity, may we and all Your people, the house of Israel, be inscribed for a good and peaceful life."

When I got home, Will was walking through the lobby with a friend, skateboards tucked under their arms. "Where were you?" he asked, casting an appraising glance at my dark suit and heavy black shoes.

"I went to services."

Will turned to his friend and said, "My Dad's Jewish."

I wasn't yet a convert, but I was curious now. It wasn't even clear to me what I was looking for—a sense of community? "I go to church because it binds me to my neighborhood and my neighbors," a Catholic friend said to me when I asked him about his faith. "I sit among congregants who I know and commune with them. It makes me feel less lonely." I knew what he meant. It comforted me to stand beside Lenny, the tallith draped over his solid shoulders; but the comfort he gave me had nothing to do with God. At this point, it was all in the family. Lenny was Dad, and I was his son.

The next spring, he and his wife, Yasmine, invited us to Passover—I hadn't been to a seder since I was a child—and we accepted, dragging along our own atheistical children. I had boned up beforehand by reading *Celebration: The Book of Jewish Festivals*, a picture book that offered a refresher course on the story of the Exodus; Lenny, a doctor who had been raised conservative, was adept at guiding us through the service. His precocious daughter, Sofia, read the Four Questions and chimed in with pertinent questions of her own. The crisp linen, the flickering candles, the plate of matzoh, the bowl with a shank bone and the bitter herbs: all this kindled in the guests a sense of collective well-being that contradicted the harsh story we were there to celebrate. Like a child being read a bedtime story, I listened rapt to the story of the Jews' deliverance from Egypt, their servitude and suffering, the plagues visited upon the pharaoh and his people, the miracle of the dividing of the Red

Sea; I drank from the cup of Mogen David as if it were a Mouton Roth-schild. I watched as the children searched for the *afikomen*—the hidden matzoh—and sang "Had Gadya" with gusto. I waited for Elijah to come through the door; and when he didn't, I was happy anyway. Who needed him? I had my family, my friends . . . everyone but God.

Still, this absence continued to nag at me—not in any consuming way, but more as a generalized absence, a longing, an equation that was somehow missing a key element. What did people do when the dark-ness seemed to swallow them up? In the bouts of desperation that, I was by this time certain—based on fifty-plus years of life and the close read-ing of alumni notes—nearly everyone experienced from time to time, I walked the streets plagued by a condition that I can only describe as spiritual isolation. Who could help me in my times of need? I had bur-dened Anna enough; my friends had their own problems; psychother-apy bored me. I wasn't a Catholic; I couldn't go sit in a confessional booth and talk to the disembodied, invisible priest through the little window.

In search of illumination, I read Paul Johnson's *History of the Jews*, a capacious and sturdy tome that weighed in at some six hundred pages and didn't have an ounce of fat. Johnson's book was exciting. It demon-strated the historicity of the Bible, invoking the papyri and artifacts that shored up his assertion—asserted by a multitude of scholars before him—that the story related in the Bible was true. The people of Israel was a real people, with a deep and ancient history, a people both perse-cuted and triumphant; they—*we*—had an existence that bound us together as a community. I was struck by the constant recourse in the Torah to this "we": "We have been stiff-necked." "We are as a passing shadow, but You are patient." "In the book of life and blessing, peace and prosperity, may we and all Your people, the house of Israel, be inscribed for a good and peaceful life." We were reviled, but we were

Chosen. It was a subversive notion in this era of cultural relativism; why should one group be "privileged" over any other? And yet it had a historical precedent. It was our tribe that had introduced monotheism to the world and established itself as unique. We had, in a sense, contributed to civilization the whole notion of identity.

It was also a contemporary story. In the wake of 9/11, the idea of being inscribed in the Book of Life ("How many shall leave this world, and how many shall be born; who shall live and who shall die, who in the fullness of years and who before") took on new meaning. As the service wound down on the second day, after the story of Jonah, after the Amidah, the long silent prayer; after the Avinu Malkeynu, recited over and over, a "catalog of petitions" to God that goes on for pages ("help us to love You with all our hearts," "keep us from being our own worst enemies"), there came the Mourner's Kaddish, recited by congregants who had suffered the death of a loved one during the last year. My father had died fourteen months before, so it was just over a year, but who was counting? I murmured the prayer: *Yit-gadal v'yit kadash . . .* How he had scoffed at religion, my father, imitating the pompous intonations of those *blebbitzing* rabbis with their platitudes about "loved ones" and the "dearly departed." Still, the words brought tears to my eyes.

One day I was walking past the monastery on Memorial Drive, across from the Charles River, in Cambridge. I had passed it many times and scarcely noticed it. It was a warm Saturday in spring, late morning. There was a signboard by the door: MIDDAY PRAYERS 12:30. I loitered by the steps in the sunshine and then—who knows why?—entered. The granite walls and wooden roof beams seemed spanking new. (So what? Even the old churches had once been new.) I sat down beneath a stained-glass window that depicted the Virgin Mary cradling the Christ

Child in her arms. A white-haired woman sitting next to me handed me a hymnal. The monks, white robed and solemn, filed in and sat down across the aisle. They opened their prayer books on their laps and began to sing:

> Father, we praise thee,
> Now the night is over, active and watchful,
> Stand we all before thee;
> Singing we offer prayer and meditation;
> Thus we adore thee.

Their voices were a monotone barely inflected by melody. Their faces, far from radiant, had a washed-out quality. But I enjoyed listening to them; it calmed me and made me think about things I rarely thought about: like *Remember how Dad and I used to rake leaves in the fall and make a big pile and burn them and watch as the sparks flew up in the chill crisp air?* and *What is my purpose here on earth?*

The service was brief, perhaps half an hour; after a final prayer from the Book of Common Prayer, the monks filed out of the chapel. As they disappeared behind a thick wooden door, I wondered about what lay on the other side of the crucifix-adorned stone wall. Did they live in bare rooms with a single cot? Did they miss the warmth of another human body in their beds? And were they more highly evolved in their spiritual lives than people in the outside world, or were they in some way unsuited to its rigors? The last monk in the queue, an elderly white-haired gentleman, looked sad. For days afterward, I wondered where he went on holidays, if he ever left the monastery. Should I write him a letter inviting him to lunch in the Square? But how would I address it? *One of the Monks, The Society of Saint John the Evangelist, 980 Memorial Drive, Cambridge, Massachusetts 02138:* "Dear white-haired guy . . ."

❖

It was the last night of the High Holidays. I had been in temple for the better part of two days. I didn't attend the whole service—I was confused about when the service *was,* and arrived too early on the last afternoon. Crossing Central Park, I noticed the rabbi sitting on a bench. To kill time, I went to the library and read magazines for an hour.

I had gone through the previous day in various states of boredom and inattention, punctuated by heightened moments of clarity and mild exaltation. One of the things I liked about the Yom Kippur service was that it addressed the difficulty of focusing one's mind. Always the daily world threatened to intrude. Prayer was work. At several junctures the congregation was enjoined to "put away commerce"—stop gnawing over that deal, why you'd allowed yourself to let the Sprint salesman who cold-called persuade you to change your service provider . . . What difference did it make in the eye of eternity? "Our origin is dust and our end is dust. At the hazard of our life we earn our bread. We are like a fragile vessel, like the grass that withers, the flower that fades, the shadow that passes, the cloud that vanishes, the wind that blows, the dust that floats, the dream that flies away." I wasn't alone in my distraction. Lenny confessed to me that he had only barely resisted the temptation to stop off at the office during the midday break to look at his e-mail. Inspired by his example, I vowed to refrain from reading e-mail on my Black-Berry, and only succumbed once.

Leafing through the Mahzor backward—I knew *that* much—I was intimidated by its length: nearly nine hundred pages, as thick as a volume of Proust. Following along on the right-hand side, where the translation was, and also the transliteration of the Hebrew, I was always scrambling to find my place. I had a million questions: Why was the rabbi wearing sneakers? (Answer: It's one of the prohibitions, Lenny whispered to me; leather is a sign of luxury. Yom Kippur is a time of repentance and purification. For the same reason you can't eat or drink or have sex.) And why were they always taking the Torah scrolls out of the Ark and then putting them back, only to take them out again later? Why couldn't they just leave them out?

Eventually I got the hang of it. (Proust wasn't always easy to get through, either.) The beauty of the language, even in the ham-handed translation of this edition, was thrilling, especially when it hewed close to the King James Bible: "God makes me lie down in green pastures and leads me beside the still waters." And I liked browsing through the stories, poems, and parables, supplemented by Talmudic commentaries from Maimonides and Nahman of Bratzlav, that adorned the text. The spirit of resistance and endurance resonated in these long-stilled voices. One of the most moving documents was a poem written by a child in the Warsaw ghetto, an inscription found on the wall of a cellar in Cologne, where Jews hid from the Nazis:

> *I believe in the sun, even when it is not shining.*
> *I believe in love, even when not feeling it.*
> *I believe in God, even when God is silent.*

The message of Yom Kippur, as it began to penetrate the carapace of my task-driven unconscious, was that we are flawed, we have sinned, we are weak; but that a solution is at hand, and that is to pray, to turn ourselves over to God, to celebrate His gorgeous Creation, and to believe that in the end, after all the travails our people have suffered, He is just. Our incessant and repetitive prayers were at once plaintive and imploring:

> *Out of the depths I call to you, O Lord.*
> *Hear my cry, O Lord;*
> *Be attentive to my plea.*

If you kept account of all sins,
O Lord, who could survive?

But with You there is forgiveness;

Therefore we revere You.

My soul yearns for the Lord
More anxiously than watchmen yearn for the dawn.

It occurred to me that we were in fact addressing "the Lord," a concept that I resisted at first. Always surly about authority, I resented the way this all-powerful God turned us into needy children: "Do not forsake us, Do not make Yourself distant from us." I was also skeptical of the prohibition against gossip. How could worshippers all over this babble-addicted city be expected to last more than a day? And the multitude of sins for which we were held accountable . . . Don't get me started.

I had acted without thinking, been guilty of foul speech, foolish talk, wanton glances, effrontery, and more. On the other hand, the exhortation to take our lives seriously intrigued me, and I liked the theme of forgiveness, the idea that you could atone for all the transgressions you'd committed during the year (though it gave me pause to learn that you were actually expected to go and apologize to the injured party; once I started down that road, I'd be working through my Rolodex into the next New Year). This God was no fool. He didn't overestimate his audience. He saw—and forgave—human frailty: "Passions, appetites, and instincts are part of our animal equipment; but whether they rule us or we rule them, we ourselves determine." (Is it any wonder that psychoanalysis is a largely Jewish profession?) I saw, too, how putting our faith in Him assuaged our earthly loneliness. The reading in unison, Lenny humming and davening beside me, gave strength.

The last hour, Neilah, "the Closing of the Gate," was tough. Older people, with canes or infirmities, were told they could sit down, but I didn't qualify for a pass yet, even by the most charitable calculation— here was one situation in which it was an advantage to be old. I stood, shifting on my feet. "It's a hard day," said Lenny: "Hard but interesting." The intensity of the rhetoric quickened ("Praised are You, Lord our God, Ruler of the Universe, Creator of the light of fire"); there were long passages of Hebrew with no English now. The dwindling number of pages in the massive book as we approached the end of the service encouraged my resolve, and my hunger focused me. In the next room I could hear the clink of cutlery as the caterers prepared for the breaking of the fast.

The shofar was sounded, the candles were lit, the congregants turned to their neighbors and declared: "Next year in Jerusalem." I stuffed a piece of whitefish in my mouth, triggering a madeleine moment; at the first taste, tart and sour, an image came to me of the delicatessen on Howard Street where I'd bicycled more than forty years before to stock up for Sunday brunch. Out on the street, in the crisp autumn wind, I checked my messages, feeling guilty (no commerce!). But I felt cleansed. *Shanah Tovah!*

Cleansed but still dissatisfied. Judaism in its historical aspect was illuminating. I now knew something about where my family was from, and the ancient tribe to which we belonged; I had a context for who, at least in my racial and ethnic makeup, I was. But I hadn't gotten to the heart of the matter; a sense of perplexity continued to nag at me. How to grasp the sheer strangeness of life? Was God simply what we called the natural world in all its weird splendor? On Sunday nights when I was watching *Nature* on PBS with the children, I would be suddenly gripped by an awareness that rationalism didn't have all the answers. An octopus with its languidly waving tentacles floating at the bottom of the sea; weird flat fish striped in every color of the rainbow; iridescent hummingbirds suspended beside a palm-size blossoming hydrangea; a stalky bulge-eyed insect on a branch: sure, evolution could account for these curious, baffling species, thrown up by the genetic luck of the draw—but not fully. If you looked at the evidence—not that I was an evolutionary biologist—the splendor of creation was more than a phrase; there lurked a question. To put it in its simplest form: how could this be?

I was channel surfing one night when I stumbled upon footage that stopped my hand on the remote. A cluster of men in many-hued robes were chanting in a pagoda-topped temple high up in the Himalayas. Some of them were playing strange instruments: six-foot-long brass horns, flutes, and drums; others brandished flags in a gorgeous tapestry of colors. On their heads were gold-peaked caps. Behind them rose bare jagged mountains.

The scene stunned me with its tranquil beauty. How far away these priests and celebrants were from the world I knew! It was heart stopping, as if I'd glimpsed a parrot flitting through dense jungle, radiant in its feathered splendor. It was a documentary about Tibet, and the next day I rushed out and bought a handful of guidebooks. I was soft, accustomed to Caribbean islands and Vermont ski resorts, but I pored over these manuals until far into the night, thrilled by the exotic itineraries. ("Approaching Zhalu from the turnoff at Khyungram, you will pass the Gyengong Lhakhang, said to be the first temple in Tibet at the Later Diffusion of Buddhism in 997.") Someday I would go there, jouncing over muddy tundra in a Land Rover with four-wheel drive, drinking yak's milk, sleeping in tents. A friend of mine had gone to Lhasa on a travel assignment and come back transformed. "I can't explain it," she said excitedly, perched on the couch in our living room one night. "The experience changes you. The way they think is not the way we think." I was open, eager to learn. I could study while I waited for the time when Will went off to college and we could embark on a long trip.

I tried to put the thought out of my mind. The very idea of a person from my background and with my temperament getting involved in something so commonplace that there was even a disparaging name for it—Jewddhism—embarrassed me. It conjured up images of Transcendental Meditationists, Hare Krishnas dancing in Washington Square Park, lost wanderers getting stoned on hashish in Kathmandu. The idea that I could meditate was laughable. I couldn't sit still for ten minutes without reaching for my cell phone.

Yet the PBS image of the monks in their temple or monastery or whatever it was stayed with me; I couldn't get rid of the sound of their music, a hypnotic blend of high-pitched horns and thumping drums that thrummed in my head as I was lying in bed or walking down the street. I was sitting at my desk one afternoon when I was seized by the impulse to call up Tibet House down in Chelsea, an institution I'd heard about—I couldn't remember where.

The receptionist at Tibet House referred me to the Shambala Center on West 22nd Street. A week later, I was ascending in the elevator to the sixth floor of a nondescript building that housed on its lower floors an assortment of accountants, no-fault divorce lawyers, and podiatrists. I had expected the center to be some mysterious grotto with incense burning and candles flickering in a darkened room, but the lobby could have been the lobby of the English department at the New School. Comfortable chairs and couches were arranged around a coffee table; the room was brightly lit, and there was a kitchen where you could raid the refrigerator for a can of Diet Coke or brew a cup of tea. The people milling around weren't freaky, either; they were dressed in down vests, T-shirts, pullovers, khakis, and jeans. They looked like graduate students. There was only one anomaly: on the floor of a closet by the door were rows of shoes. Everyone was padding around in socks. I took off my loafers and put them in the closet.

I asked a receptionist where the beginner's meditation instruction was held, and she pointed me to a gym-size room with square red pillows set on mats on the shiny wood floor. There were seven other people there, seated cross-legged on their pillows. The instructor came in and sat down on a cushion at the front of the room. His blond hair was cut short, and he had on a blue button-down shirt. I guessed that he was around thirty-five. He could have been a high school chemistry teacher. "Greetings. I'm Robert, and this is Beginning Meditation," he said in a nearly inaudible voice. "I thought perhaps we could begin by going around the room and introducing yourself and saying a little bit about what brought you here."

Robert nodded at a young man in a green hospital orderly's uniform. "My name is Leon, and I guess I got interested in Buddhism after hearing the Dalai Lama speak in Central Park last summer. There was this huge crowd, and there was something . . ." He paused, searching for the right words. "Something about the way he, like, calmed everyone down that really impressed me. It was like he had some, I don't know, knowledge. I just wanted to know more."

Robert went around the room, nodding at each person in turn. There was a child psychologist who had been reading up on Buddhism; a woman with a gaunt face and long dark hair that flowed down around her shoulders who described herself as "an artist"; an older woman in a bulky sweater who said she wasn't "doing much of anything right now"; a serious-looking man in a leather jacket who spoke about a trip to India he'd taken that awoke his curiosity about the Buddha. Robert thanked him and nodded at me. I couldn't think of anything to say. "I . . . I . . ." I stared at the floor. "I'm a writer, and I was never religious, but I got interested in Judaism late in life because . . . I needed help,

some explanation . . ." Of what? I couldn't explain my need for an explanation, or what it was that I needed to have explained. "Anyway . . ." I
trailed off. "So here I am." Nice, Jim. That was really eloquent.

To Robert, it was apparently a satisfactory, even moving, answer. It
was as if I had bared my soul to its very depths, gotten at some deep
mystery.

He explained the practice of meditation. First the basics: you had to
find a position that was comfortable for you, whether it was sitting
cross-legged with your hands on your knees or in your lap, or knees up,
arms clasped around them, or whatever. The important thing was to sit.
To sit and not do anything but observe your thoughts as they passed
by—the image that came into my mind was the stock ticker tape in
Times Square. "The object is not to get rid of thoughts, but to see them
as thoughts. Don't try to suppress them—you can't anyway. They're like
gophers—you smash down one and whoops, there's another one." We
laughed. "Thoughts are transitory; they stream by and can't be fixed in
the mind. When you see a person walking down the street talking to
himself you think, 'That person is crazy.' But when you walk down the
street what are you thinking about? You're thinking about what happened in the past or what's going to happen in the future—something
you did wrong at work, something you're going to do to get a promotion. But the past and the future are as unreal as the madman's halluci-
nations. The past is over and can't be changed, the future hasn't happened yet. So what are you talking to yourself about?" He sat in silence
for a while.

"This is why we focus on the breath. When you become aware of
yourself breathing, it means that you've come back from thinking about
all the stuff you've been thinking about. You've come back to the center
of yourself. You're not trying to achieve peace, you're not trying to control your thoughts. You're just *there.*" Pause. "There's no such thing as a

bad meditator. You can realize that you're having a sex fantasy and think, 'Oh, there's a good way to kill fifteen minutes . . .'" We laughed. "But it doesn't matter. You have all these thoughts: 'I forgot my umbrella in the rain; I'm late; I've got to go to Whole Foods after this meeting and pick up some groceries'—which is what I'm going to do." More laughter. "Eventually, once you've trained yourself, you'll come back to the breath. You'll feel yourself breathing. You'll feel yourself *be*."

On the floor beside him was a gong in the shape of an inverted bell, a sheepskin-swathed baton leaning against its inner wall like a king-size mortar and pestle. Robert picked up the baton and lightly struck the gong. It vibrated for a long time, the sound dying off almost imperceptibly.

I sat on my cushion feeling incredibly foolish. What on earth was I doing here? Anna was at home with Molly and Will eating Chinese food from Ollie's Noodle Shop; their dad was sitting in a room with a bunch of strangers, cross-legged on the floor like a kindergartner listening to his teacher read a story ("And goodnight moon"). Why not seek solace from my well-thumbed copy of Dr. Johnson's *Selected Writings*? I would have been just as edified; there was a whole separate section called "Prayers." ("Almighty and most merciful Father, who lovest those whom thou punishest, look down with pity upon my sorrows . . .")

The sound of the gong awoke me from my reverie. I opened my eyes. My six fellow meditators sat quietly on their cushions. Robert nodded at us and explained that we bow at the end of the session "to show our gratitude to the Buddha." He put his hands together in prayer and bowed. We put our hands together and bowed. Then I got up and went to find my shoes.

On a table in the lobby were books on Buddhism for sale. On my way out, I bought a book called *The Art of Happiness: A Handbook for Living*, by His Holiness the Dalai Lama. I read it over the next few days, carrying it with me everywhere—on the bus, in taxis, as I lay in bed late at night. I couldn't believe I was reading this book. *The Art of Happiness:* how hackneyed could you get. Siddhartha on the subway. Millions of people had read this book—millions of lost souls. Losers. I had spent my life reading the Great Books—or, lately, *about* the great books. Literature, as I'd studied and absorbed it over a lifetime, was about skepticism, disenfranchisement and dislocation, failed and ruined lives. Life, in short, was tragic: that was the message of my favorite novelists—Flaubert, Tolstoy, Conrad, Joyce. Now I was reading a book that said the purpose of life was to achieve happiness. Good luck.

I was skeptical of the Dalai Lama's teachings. I couldn't subscribe to his dictum that "chasing after the five worldly pleasures—running after fame, wealth, sex, sleep, or food" wasn't the road to enlightenment. I was convinced that if I managed to obtain the five worldly pleasures—I already had the last three, but the first two were proving stubbornly elusive—I might not even need God. And he failed to explain how you were supposed to survive those moments when, as a friend of mine who had been fired from his job at the age of fifty-seven said, "I thought I would fall down in the street"—moments that called forth, in their demand of ordinary, uncelebrated courage, the heroism of everyday life. Where was God when you needed Him?

The Dalai Lama's advice on such crises of the spirit, as far as I could tell, was to see our suffering as a lesson in the transitory nature of existence, the impermanence of all things. His insistence on playing down the value of the self, which he saw as a hindrance to enlightenment, appealed to me; it echoed Eliot's assertion that only those afflicted with a personality knew what it meant to crave its extinction. And I endorsed his plea for heightened consciousness, the elimination of negative emotions, the cultivation of Mindfulness. Negativity, the Dalai Lama taught, interferes with our quest for centeredness and inner balance; it blocks our access to Right

Views, Right Thought, Right Speech . . . and so on. Put bluntly, we were meant to internalize basic human values—to own them, as it were. Only then would we be ready to know God (or whatever in Buddhism passed for God; I was never too clear on this point). But wasn't the point of those colossal churches built stone by stone over centuries in Europe to transcend the limits of nature and celebrate the infinite power of God? The trouble with Buddhism was that it was *too much* of this world.

A friend to whom I had confided my theological quandary gave me a book by a New York psychoanalyst named Barry Magid called *Ordinary Mind: Exploring the Common Ground of Zen and Psychotherapy.* Having stomped on this common ground—at least on the psychotherapy side—until it was worn down to bare earth, I seized upon Magid's book with a college-student ardor. Here was self-insight combined with spiritual enlightenment: the ultimate twofer. A practicing psychotherapist, Magid was familiar with the ways in which we thwart ourselves through anger and self-destructive behavior. His solution was not to repair the fragile self but to banish it. "Neurosis doesn't evaporate into thin air," Magid cautioned. "Our tendency to be frustrated or narcissistically injured will dramatically decrease when our practice reveals we have no essential self to defend." And as we learn to dwell less on our achievements, our possessions, our preoccupation with status and identity, we open up space for the spiritual life—which in Zen is synonymous with the life of this world. Magid offered up a parable:

A monk said to Chao-chou, "I have just entered the monastery. Please teach me."

Chao-chu said, "Have you eaten your rice gruel?"

The monk said, "Yes, I have."

Chao-chou said, "Wash your bowl." The monk understood.

So did I, more or less. What Chao-chou was saying was that enlightenment came to us only when we accepted things as they were, an acceptance measured by our willingness to go about our daily tasks without great expectations. The way to spiritual centeredness was not to want.

On the way to Vermont, I would pass a ramshackle gray-shingled house on a main road that had a sign in front: THE BODHI TREE INN DHARMA CENTER. I was often tempted to pull into the driveway and knock on the door. Who lived there? How had they ended up in this house and how did they live? Did they have more peace of mind than I did? And—a more mundane but still crucial question—how did they get by? Did they pump gas at the local Mobil station? Did they have trust funds? At bad moments in my life, I fantasized about giving up my worldly goods and joining the band of invisible Buddhists in their dispiriting house. I would slow down and try to get a glimpse of them through the windows, but I never saw anyone—the shades were drawn or the occupants had gone to the local Wal-Mart. (Was it still okay to go to Wal-Mart after you'd attained enlightenment?) It was with a sense of relief that I hit the accelerator and sped away from that creepy haunted house.

I enrolled in a yoga class and quit after one session, exasperated by the teacher, an anorexic-thin young woman with frizzy hair that spiked from her head as if she'd just put her finger in an electric socket; she barked orders at me on a chilly squash court, stood over me as if I were some accident victim, and pushed my limbs about. ("Okay, now twist your spine, move your right hand down to clasp your left ankle and tuck your right foot under your left buttock: this is known as Ardha Matsyendrasana, Lord of the Fishes.") Her exhortations to relax made me tense. It was only when we sat cross-legged on our rubber mats at the end of the session and observed five minutes of silence—she, too, sounded a gong—that I felt a fleeting calm.

In a brochure I'd picked up at the Shambala Center was a schedule of weekly dharma gatherings held on Tuesday nights at seven. These were lectures on various aspects of Buddhism. "Samsara: No, It's Not a Perfume. It's a Snake." "The Guru: Someone to Worship? That Holy-looking Guy in the Robes Wants Your Money." "Enlightenment: What Is It? Who's Got It? How Do I Get It?" I decided to go back.

When I arrived on a cold November night, all the cushions were occupied. I took a seat on a folding chair off to the side. In back of me was a table that had little shrines on it—Buddhas, gold cups, porcelain vases. On the wall were photographs of *rinpoches*—*rinpoche* is the Tibetan word meaning "guru"—their frames draped in brightly colored scarves. There was a row of glasses filled with water. I picked up a glass and took a sip. The woman next to me, a wraith with close-cropped purple-dyed hair, whispered urgently, "Don't do that! That's for the Buddha." I put the glass back on the table, as guilty as if I'd been caught by a cashier swiping a Snickers bar.

The speaker that night was a man named John Baker. He was bald, maybe a few years older than me, and had a kindly, composed face. I was reassured by his tie and jacket. John spoke with great ease, only rarely consulting the piece of paper in his lap. He had been a Buddhist for thirty years and had received his training at the Naropa Institute in Boulder, Colorado, under the supervision of a monk named Chongyam Trungpa, *rinpoche*. Chongyam Trungpa had fled the Chinese when they invaded Tibet, gone to India, then migrated to Oxford and, after a period of solitary meditation at a retreat in Bhutan, married a young Englishwoman and come to America, where he founded the institute. He had died at the age of forty-seven. (Later on, I read a book about the Naropa Institute that described Chongyam Trungpa as an unashamed hedonist who liked to smoke, drink, and chase women, which kind of freaked me out; I wanted him to be pure, monklike in his saffron robes, not just another foreigner intent on Westernization.

But maybe that was part of Buddhism: living with imperfection, tolerating disillusionment. People were the way they were.)

"Every one of us on this planet thinks we're special," John began. "Every one of us thinks that what we're doing, how we live, whether we have a loved one or a partner or children or live alone, work or don't work—*whatever we do*—is of the greatest importance. But imagine that you're looking at the planet from Mars. You can't even see your house." Laughter. "There are eight billion people on the planet, and each one feels that his life is of the greatest importance. There are dogs; each dog feels that its life is important. Elephants. Giraffes—not as many as there used to be, but still . . . If you have a garden, there are millions of insects in the garden going about their work of eating up your plants." Laughter. "They're all important and not important. They just are. Buddhism isn't a negative religion. It doesn't teach that everything is meaningless, that you should empty your mind. It teaches you to go outside yourself and *see*."

Some of John's directives seemed familiar—perhaps too familiar: "We want to be there for our own lives now." "We need to sit down and figure out who we are and not bring down chaos on our lives and the lives of others." "Experience is beyond language." "What we call the self is a fiction." It was the *way* he talked that I found so compelling. "Buddhism is about the examination of one's experience, understanding our relationship to the world we live in," he said. And that's what he tried to help us do. When he told a funny story, he laughed with us, sharing the joke; when he told a somber story, he did it without sounding pious. "A famous *rinpoche* came to this country for the first time," he recounted one night, "and his host took him to the observation tower at the top of the Empire State Building. As the *rinpoche* stood looking out over the city, he began to weep. 'Why are you weeping?' asked the host. 'I'm weeping to think of the millions of people who are suffering and have no one to comfort them.'" John looked around the room. "That is why we come here, out of suffering, confusion, and pain."

I kept going back to the Shambala Center. The room was generally full when I got there at seven. Whatever the weather—snowstorms or downpours or Arctic cold—I'd walk through the double doors into the meditation room and see the backs of a hundred silent people sitting cross-legged on cushions. Outside I could hear the muffled noises of New York—car alarms, sirens, the roar and grind of garbage trucks. Even in the lobby people swirled and babbled as if they were at a cocktail party. The people on their cushions were oblivious, lost in thought—or the absence of thought.

Sometimes I felt sad when I first settled down in the meditation room. What was I doing here? I wasn't the oldest person in the room; a woman who wore her hair in a bun and had a Quaker air about her and a sixtyish man with a white ponytail came every week. The man had a weather-beaten face, as if he'd slept outdoors on a sidewalk grate at some point in his life. But it seemed kind of pathetic anyway. The image that came to my mind as I sat on a cushion in the pinstripe suit I'd worn to work, my tie stowed in my pocket, was of a guy in a raincoat sitting at the bar of one of those grotto-like Irish dives on Second Avenue in the middle of the day.

But I found that I liked meditating. When I sat down, I knew that for the next half hour no one would talk to me, meaning no one would have the opportunity to hurt or reject me. I was disappearing into a world that was mine alone. I took to meditating at home for fifteen minutes a day, the way I'd been told. I would grab a cushion off the couch in the bedroom, close the door, and plump myself down on the floor. Beside me was my wristwatch and a pair of bronze bells that I got from a Tibetan store next to the Hertz garage on West 77th Street for twenty dollars; they were shaped like a coolie's hat and attached to each other by a leather shoelace. They were so beautiful, with their carved writhing serpents and Tibetan letters; I had to discipline myself to ring them only at the beginning of the session and at the end. "Sometimes he rings the bells once," Will reported to Anna, "but sometimes he's just Dad, and he starts ringing them like crazy."

Even if, as Robert maintained, there was no such thing as a bad meditator, I felt myself becoming more skilled. I still couldn't figure out the difference between the Hinayana and the Mahayana, the Sevenfold Puja and the Eightfold Path, but when I ended a session I felt more at ease with myself, lighter. "When you practice, observe how much peace, happiness, and lightness you already have," writes Thich Nhat Hanh in *Teachings on Love,* an addition to the growing shelf of Buddhist texts piled up on my bedside table. "Notice whether you are anxious about accidents or misfortunes, and how much anger, irritation, fear or worry are already in you." Thich, you don't know the half of it.

When I closed the door and banged my coolie's-hat gongs together, I was happy. In the beginning the usual stuff clogged my mind: *My MasterCard is a thousand plus overdrawn, so why did I buy those hiking boots I saw in the window of Edmonds when the pair I have is fine? Did Bruce actually not speak to me in the elevator or was I just imagining it? Was . . . Why . . . Who . . .* The first five minutes was like working through the rules I'd learned in journalism for writing the lead. Gradually, though, I would become aware that I was thinking of other things: *I am here now but just passing through; I won't be here for long.* That wasn't exactly news: I already knew from my Judaic studies that our origin is dust and our end is dust, but it was interesting to encounter it in this new form. *Why did I blurt out . . . ?* What, back so soon? Don't you know *the past is past? The whole point is that you have to be in your own center and not expect some external person or situation to act for you. In other words, he who develops highly skilled patience will never expect anything from anyone, not because he is distrustful, but because he knows how to be at the center and he is the center. So will you let it go already? He's not saying it's all about you. He's saying you should be independent. It's for you to determine the meaning of what has happened to you; it's for you to determine your own future and what it will mean. Remember that crazy Baba Ram Dass you used to make fun of when you were stoned in college? Be Here Now. But he was right: nowness sharpens your experience of life.*

I had a problem with some of what Chongyam Trungpa said. *I do not exist; the external visualization does not exist; the act of visualizing does not exist.* I do exist, I protested. Who else is this longing for a Ding Dong from the deli across the street? *Even the tree loves you.* The tree does not love me. *If someone wants something that you have, you should give it to them.* No way. *But what if he's saying the things of this world can't make you happy. Possessions can only get you so far.*

My time was up. I didn't have an alarm clock. Somehow I'd gotten to know intuitively when fifteen minutes had elapsed. I opened my eyes and glanced at my watch. Seventeen minutes. The time had passed quickly.

One night after his talk I went up to John Baker and asked him a question. He had been talking about ego and ambition, how ambition gets in the way of our ability to just live. "We're so focused on getting somewhere that we miss the details, so you have to be careful about ambition," he'd said. "Every instant of one's life could be art." This bothered me. I was willing to sit here on my cushion and learn to think about life in a new way; but did that mean I had to give up my ambition? There was still so much I wanted to do. In some ways I felt I was just beginning to come into my own.

I cornered John as he came out of the hall. "Can I ask you about something you said in your talk that I had trouble with?"

He looked at me and smiled. I was struck by his patience. Instead of being eager to get to the tea and cookies that waited on a table in the hall, he was giving me his full attention. "Say you're ambitious. Does that mean you can't write a big book or try to advance in your career?" I said.

John thought a moment. "Ambition gets in the way of creativity, don't you think?" He smiled gently and put his hand on my shoulder. "Let's go get some cookies before they're all gone."

The parable of the novice who asks the monk for enlightenment and the monk says "Wash your bowl" flew into my head. Do your work. Don't think about where it will get you. Just do it. *Wash your bowl.*

On my way out, I noticed a photograph pasted to a chopstick on the altar by the door. The chopstick was stuck in a bowl of rice. I went over and studied the photograph. It was of a man with rimless glasses and a trim beard. He was smiling at the camera. At the bottom of the photograph was a handwritten note:

Jan Augustson
January 18, 1949—December 19, 2003

Two months older than me. When he died, was he enlightened? Would anyone know the difference when he was under the ground or in his urn? I tried to remind myself that death was simply a part of life. I was here, then I wouldn't be here. What I did on earth mattered, but not all that much.

I got my shoes out of the closet, bought another book from the cashier at the table in the lobby—*The Path Is the Goal: A Basic Handbook of Buddhist Meditation*—and headed down in the elevator. Outside, I started to unfurl my umbrella. It had been pouring when I arrived, but the rain had stopped and the air felt cleansed. The rain-slicked pavement shone in the light from a streetlamp.

I went out onto Sixth Avenue and hailed a taxi. I was eager to get home.

Twenty-fifth Anniversary

Eleanor looks troubled when she arrives at the door. "I have something to tell you," she says as she sits down at the kitchen table. "Wally and I are getting divorced."

I'm stunned—for the fourth time this year. Over the next hour, the familiar tale unfolds—familiar yet unfamiliar. Each permutation is different. The most common is the man leaving the family for another, inevitably younger woman; but there are other surprising variations: the man leaving for another man, the woman leaving for another woman, the man or woman leaving not for someone else but . . . just because. Every time, I say to Anna: "I had no idea. They seemed so happy."

What happened was this: Wally had lost his job at the publishing house where he'd worked for a decade, and he'd had trouble finding a new one. He was sitting around at home all day while Eleanor went off to work as a senior editor at a women's magazine. "Then one day I came home and he had this solemn look on his face. He had to talk to me. 'There's someone else . . .' That line."

Why now? Why, as we pass the critical fifty mark, are peoples' marriages unraveling at such a startling rate? For two decades, divorces in our circle were remarkably infrequent. There were one or two early on, not long after our friends started getting married—first-time mistakes. And there were others a few years ago: Larry getting a jump on the midlife crisis, Ted bailing because he felt like "fucking a lot of women."

My theory is that people—especially men—hit a wall around fifty. They've accomplished a lot, or a little, but there's nowhere else in the work hierarchy to go, no next step on the ladder; or the dream job they landed twenty years ago has lost its novelty. There's a sense of shrinking horizons, of possibilities closing down. Life seems static, uneventful; the end of the road is in sight. What better way to shake things up than to tear your life apart in the name of freedom—find a fresh source of adoration, someone new to listen adoringly to the old stories?

There's an opposite scenario: too much success. "We got divorced when we could afford to," Jules Feiffer said of his generation—largely Bronx- and Brooklyn-born intellectuals who made the journey over the bridge to Manhattan hand in hand with a spouse from the same background. As they rose in the world, their social and sexual expectations rose with them. The first wife got shunted off to the side. When they had begun their lives together, they were practically kids. Then they came of age—not always in the same way.

Disparities in development start to manifest themselves—and it's not always the man who pulls ahead. Sometimes a woman's career takes off. In one couple I know, the wife became a famous writer while the husband, also a writer, couldn't get his novel published. Money becomes a problem, especially if the wife begins to make more. We're not sufficiently evolved as a culture so that the stay-at-home dad is regarded as a courageous, march-to-his-own-drummer kind of guy.

Every marriage, Phyllis Rose writes in *Parallel Lives,* is "a narrative construct, a subjectivist fiction with two points of view often deeply in conflict, sometimes fortuitously congruent." What makes for this congruency? A marriage "in which the two parties agree on the scenario they are enacting." But that scenario can change over time. It's impossible when we're thirty to know how we'll have evolved by forty. It's luck if it works. What if one party has become a convert to Buddhism and the other is obsessed with getting ahead at the investment bank? What if one talks to Mom on the phone every day and drags the family over to the parents' house for Sunday dinner, while the other, a child of clinging parents, wants nothing more than to break away from all familial obligations?

I have friends (especially women; men are more needy) who've decided they no longer need spouses. Married women end up doing two jobs: the laundry, the shopping, the cooking—plus taking care of their husbands, an additional chore. What's in it for them? Unsettling developments in biology and social *moeurs*—in vitro fertilization, marriage between lesbians—have created scenarios in which men would simply become irrelevant. (I'm not against this in principle, provided it happens a few generations down the line. Just think: no more war, no more SUVs polluting the atmosphere, no deforestation, no crime.) We can move furniture, fix the plumbing, carry suitcases: that's about it. I suspect that a lot of women would rather cope with the stigma of singlehood than drag around some feeble husband for the rest of their lives. Some women I know possess such interesting minds that they don't need anyone else around to entertain them—it's as if they're married to themselves. They won't admit it, since the supposedly natural condition of single women is to be forever hunting for a mate. The hero of *Bridget Jones's Diary* frets endlessly about her unattached state but secretly appears to enjoy it. (I've interviewed the author, Helen Fielding, in her posh digs off Carnaby Street, and she didn't give off an aura of pathos.) If they're tough-minded enough, they *do* admit it. "Maybe I wasn't made to be married," Daphne Merkin wrote in *The New Yorker*, reviewing a collection of books on marriage. "Maybe I'm fated to be alone." Besides, married men live longer than single men, but single women—provided they're divorced or widowed—live longer than women who have married. We're dangerous to our wives' health.

There's also the boomer/narcissicism factor. Marriage requires sacrifices—if you're lucky, minor ones. In her biting polemic, *Against Love*, Laura Kipnis catalogs the disharmonies that can disrupt a marriage: "You can't eat what you want: good-bye Marshmallow Fluff, hello tofu meatballs. You can't not eat meals. You can't not have dinner together. You can't bring Ding Dongs into the house . . ." And so on for pages, a Homeric list of prohibitions. Our generation doesn't react well to the idea of sacrifice. We're impatient with the delicate negotiations required to sustain a marriage. I know a person who walked out on his wife because she expected him to be faithful. "I've been faithful for twenty-three years," he told her. "That's long enough."

In my parents' generation, people didn't get divorced as readily as they do now. Frank Rich, in his memoir *Ghost Light*, writes about how isolating and strange it was to have divorced parents in the 1950s. "I was different, in a family unlike any other family I knew in life or on television." He writes: "Our family was now defined by that two-syllable word, almost a second name, that was uttered—in my presence, at least—only in the whisper that Grandma Rose used when talking about being Jewish or having cancer: *divorce*."

My parents' marriage lasted sixty-four years—until death did them part. And none of their friends got divorced, either: not one couple in their entire circle. Does this mean they all had happy marriages? Doubtful: who knows what crises punctuated their long lives together? Not long ago I learned that my handsome, dashing grandfather apparently had an affair with his secretary. And one hears rumors of other infidelities among those long dead. But it was customary to stay together. In some cases—my own parents are an example—conflicts that would now precipitate divorce were endured, with the result that couples who had gone through "a bad patch" sometimes grew back together and became harmonious. My parents were happiest together in their seventies and eighties, when their struggles had been put behind them. Old age—even middle age—can be a time of bitterness, the lost chance for marital concord forever beyond retrieval; but it can also be a time of reconciliation, when past sins and hurts inflicted begin to fade away. "After loving you so much, can I forget / you for eternity, and have no other choice?" Robert Lowell wrote in a poem to his wife Elizabeth in the last year of his life, looking back at their inordinately stormy union—which only ended when he died in a taxi returning to her after the collapse of another marriage.

On the other hand, some marriages that dissolve, through death or divorce, are better off dissolved. I've seen friends blossom when they finally got rid of a deadbeat mate. A friend of mine whose husband ran off with a twentysomething-year-old wept bitterly for two weeks and then resumed her morning run, her novel, her life. She went out more. The end of a marriage can be the beginning of a new life. The cocoon of your marriage breaks open. You're free. "When I'm with my girlfriend I don't think about death," confides a journalist I know who walked out on his wife of twenty-seven years. Another, long in a suffocating marriage, likes his new walk-up; reduced circumstances don't outweigh the benefits of hitting the Third Avenue bars in search of fresh—let me find a decorous word—companionship. Who says you have to stay married for life? In earlier centuries, people didn't live long enough to rack up forty, fifty, sixty years of marriage. The idea that you could end up spending that many years together barely occurred to anyone.

The argument is often made that monogamy is unnatural. Males have to spread their sperm around in order to maximize the chances of reproduction. DNA drives the behavior of the species—except, I gather, in the case of the monogamous vole. Maybe the bonds of matrimony are fraying because monogamy is simply unsustainable. Can the spate of divorces among my friends, the willingness to scratch the "till death do us part" clause, be in fact a reversion to the norm? Monogamy is a recent historical development. In antiquity, in Renaissance Europe, in England during the seventeenth and eighteenth centuries or Victorian England, monogamy wasn't a virtue. Marriage was a social or economic arrangement; it had nothing to do with fidelity, or even love. An unhappy marriage wasn't considered grounds for divorce—which was why it was so rare. Elizabeth Cady Stanton, the leader of the nineteenth-century suffragette movement, dragged around an incompatible husband through four decades of marriage and seven children.

Even today, attitudes toward marriage are more casual in Europe than here. My English friends have nearly all been divorced—some multiple times. My address book is strewn with crossed-out names and addresses of jettisoned spouses. When Anna, at a London dinner party, mentioned in passing that she'd been married for twenty-five years, her table companion, a prominent writer, gasped in horror. And look at France, with its tradition of lovers and mistresses. At Mitterand's funeral, the wife sat on one side of the aisle, the mistress on the other. Who cared? Europeans regard Americans as absurdly puritanical, and maybe we are; have we created a social regimen that stifles our freedom and makes us resentful?

It could be argued that the prevalence of divorce among my generation is a legacy of the 1960s, a repudiation of authority, a throwing off of sexual chains. Just do it. Still, I can't help wondering if this solution to marital discord, and the de-stigmatizing of it, has negative consequences—jealousy, for instance, destruction of trust, loss of the deep connection forged by obedience to vows. And let's be practical: the suspension of all customs brings with it a certain amount of wear and tear—shuffling children around, fighting in court, building bunk beds for the kids in cramped new quarters. A friend whose marriage was tottering reported to me the advice he'd gotten from another newly divorced friend of ours: "Don't get divorced if you can help it. It's a cold world out there."

Thirty years ago, when all of us were getting married, we were as oblivious to the idea of divorce as we were to the idea of infidelity, job loss, failure, bodily decline, and death. The brides were radiant in their white gowns, the grooms solemn in their new suits. The band played; waiters in black bow ties and black vests circulated with flutes of champagne on silver trays in the tents; we sat at round tables covered with snowy tablecloths and dined on plates of rare roast beef and asparagus with béchamel sauce; the children scampered across the green lawns; the evening came and the sky grew dark and the stars came out and the bride and groom disappeared in a hail of rice and the guests trailed out to their cars and drove off into the night. "Helen looked radiant, don't you think?" we said as we undid our cuff links and pulled off our shoes. "They're lucky they found each other."

What about sex? Sometimes a marriage goes sour because the couple is bored in bed. (I've always wondered if this is what divorce lawyers refer to as "irreconcilable differences.") "I mount my wife," writes John Cheever in his journal, tersely summing up the cheerless nature of his conjugal duties. It's a commonly held view that nothing interesting happens between couples who have been together for a long time—especially in bed. Children, jobs, domestic obligations can sap a long marriage of its juices. "It was all like clockwork," complains the dutiful husband in Bergman's *Scenes from a Marriage*—"hermetically sealed off, neatly arranged."

Children don't help matters. Sex has to be scheduled around their intermittent absences: *Quick! Tommy's at baseball practice. Let's go.* In the early stages of child raising especially, they desexualize us. The mother becomes "Mom," the father becomes "Dad." The mother sterilizes the baby bottles in a sauce pot on the stove, the father—if he's one of the new liberated or "feminized" men, not just some *schlub* slumped in front of the TV watching the Super Bowl with a cold Bud clutched in his hand—does the laundry and folds the sheets. Slaving away as a "team," we forget what brought us together in the first place. All we know is that a staff of two is required.

But what if your spouse *is* interesting? Jonathan Yardley, in his memoir of his parents' lifelong marriage, *Our Kind of People,* noted their "ardent physical attraction to each other." They were both virgins when they married and regularly consulted a marital handbook entitled *Sex Habits,* which seems to have done the trick. "Their physical relations were ecstatic, frequent, and imaginative," Yardley reports. (What did they do? And how does he know?) Joyce wrote Nora the dirtiest letters in the language: "My love for you allows me to pray to the spirit of eternal beauty and tenderness mirrored in your eyes or to fling you down under me on that soft belly of yours and fuck you up behind, like a hog riding a sow, glorying in the very stink and sweat that rises from your arse." He gazed longingly at other women and filled his notebook with fantasies about a student in Trieste whom he taught at Berlitz: "I hold the websoft edges of her gown and drawing them out to hook them I see through the opening of the black veil her little body sheathed in an orange shift." But it was all in his head. Where it remained.

"You never know the truth about anyone else's marriage." The familiar axiom might be amended: "Especially a good one." The bad marriage is often a public spectacle: fighting at dinner parties, never being seen together, a flagrant adulterous liaison. (Though often it's not: behind the public facade of geniality are all manner of fissures.) Good marriages tend to be private. "If it's good you don't want to jinx things by talking about it in public," says a friend who has been happily married for a long time, "and if it's bad you don't want to say so."

The domestic idiosyncracies of two lives shared so intensely would strike those outside the fortress of their intimacy as eccentric. "How is it, my darling, that you say you have broken the habit of expectoration?" writes John Stuart Mill to his wife, Harriet. We know what's in the other's medicine cabinet, their bathroom rituals, what the doctor said, what each one likes to eat, the type of underwear preferred, how they really feel about their friends, the millions of words exchanged day and night. "What can come between us now?" Joyce wrote to Nora. "We have suffered and been tried. Every veil of shame or diffidence seems to have fallen from us. Will we not see in each other's eyes the hours and hours of happiness that are waiting for us?"

It's to each other that the long-married confide. Like Kitty and Levin in *Anna Karenina* (as fascinating a couple, to my mind, as those adulterers Vronsky and Anna), the long-married utter their thoughts "boldly, without taking the trouble to clothe them in exact language." They intuit each other's responses: like the joke about prisoners long pent up, they can invoke no. 47 (Getting lost: "Doesn't it remind you of the time we got lost in the Lake District during that torrential rainstorm?"). This convocation of identical thoughts is sometimes embarrassing. Driving through the ghastly wasteland of New Jersey on the way to visit friends in Princeton, I begin my familiar lament about how beautiful the world must have been before the rise of industrialism. Anna puts up two fingers in a cross: time-out. Been there, heard that.

"Do you remember how we decided to get married?" she says one night over pasta in our neighborhood Italian restaurant.

I do, but I speak my part. Does Ralph Fiennes as Hamlet during a long run at the Belasco turn to the audience and explain that he's decided to omit his "To be or not to be" soliloquy because he said it last night?

JIM: We were at that Greek restaurant on Mass. Ave. What's its name?
ANNA: The Parthenon.
JIM: Right. The Parthenon. I can even remember what you were wearing: a red turtleneck.
ANNA: Wasn't it strange how we just knew?
JIM: I still don't know what you saw in me. Didn't I talk the whole night about structuralism?
ANNA: No, I think it was the Frankfurt School. You were obsessed with Walter Benjamin.
JIM (correcting her pronunciation): Ben-ya-mean.

The waiter arrives bearing plates of moussaka. The curtain falls.

It gives us pleasure to recite our lines. We like to invoke that transformative moment when—after much confusion and two years apart—we realized our marital destiny. It was fortuitous—it could have easily not happened. Back from a fellowship abroad, I was kicking around a big house in Boston, at loose ends, unemployed, unattached. A mutual friend told me Anna was in town, taking some courses. Burned by my previous relationship, which had flamed out with maximum pain, I was reluctant to get involved again. My friend, over beers at a bar on the waterfront, again suggested I call her. So I did. There followed the dinner at the Greek restaurant. What if I hadn't had drinks with my friend? I hate to think.

Anna and I raised each other. Looking back, as we often do, we remember the very young people we were, unsure of how to dress, how to decorate an apartment, how to behave at family get-togethers; we lived in Cambridge apartments with no furniture, stayed in down-at-the-heels European hotels. We taught each other all the basic things our parents, distracted by problems of their own, hadn't taught us to do. "What kind of dress do you wear to a cocktail party?" Anna would say, rummaging through her closet. And I, groping my way through the early stages of adult life, unable to recognize an oyster fork; ignorant of the fact that you have to put the butter on your butter plate, not just slather it directly onto your roll; unaware that shirts without button-down collars require stays: it was Anna who instructed me, calling upon a store of information acquired from random sources she couldn't quite identify.

I like to read about couples who left the world as they had lived in it—together. Bruce and Naomi Bliven, staff writers for *The New Yorker*, died a week apart; William Maxwell and his wife, Emily, another married pair of staff writers at the magazine, died within a few months of each other. "Two people can never live beside each other in perfect intimacy," Maxwell said not long before he died—or rather, they died. His wife never told him that her illness was fatal. But they shared their dying as they did their lives. Philip and Anna Hamburger were still another *New Yorker* couple in for the long haul. (What is it about that magazine that promotes longevity? Is it the healthy sense of belonging to a larger family that nurtures and protects them from the identity-threatening tumult of the outside world?) "Phil and Anna were a couple in the gin-and-tonic, Heloise-and-Abelard sense," recalled their friend Roger Angell in a "Talk of the Town" piece: "You rarely thought of them as anything but two—he in his dark suit, with his curved little smile; she close at hand, with pale lipstick and extraordinary hair.'"

It's our twenty-fifth wedding anniversary, and we've arranged a little party in the carriage barn of the Victorian house in our Vermont town where we got married on the hottest day any local could remember. It was August that long-ago day, and 102 degrees. The ceremony was held in the garden. We were twenty-six and so clueless that we forgot to order chairs; the guests stood in a cluster while the minister guided us through our vows. I remember Anna's wedding dress, and my brown cord suit—the first one I ever owned. How thin she was, and still thin now, twenty-five years later. I've thickened; the suit is long gone. (I can still stuff myself into the tuxedo I bought in 1986 if I take a deep breath and hold it in when I'm fastening the trousers.) We toast each other, lifting our flutes of champagne.

After supper, we dance to a local band, refugee hippies who never left town, the fiddle and acoustic guitar filling the barn. Everyone is on the dance floor: Jon and Susan; Fred and Mac; Steve and Robin; the kids; our newly divorced neighbor, Eleanor; even my mom and dad. (He has a year to go.) They totter among the tables, holding on to each other for dear life.

It's nearly midnight when the last guests straggle off to the bed-and-breakfast down the road. The night air has a late-August sharpness to it, a chill that portends the arrival of autumn. We've gone through half an adult lifetime. Sometimes our wedding day seems like ancient history—pre-children, pre-career, pre-everything. Sometimes it seems like yesterday. An image comes to me of Molly and William playing beside a pond in the garden, trying to capture a toad; not too many years from now they'll be getting married at this house, and we'll be the ones sitting in chairs on the lawn. (We'll know to *have* chairs.)

The caterers are putting away the tables and loading up their truck. We drive back to the farmhouse and get ready for bed—the same bed we slept in the night before the wedding. I've brought back a piece of cake on a paper plate, and we eat it with a plastic fork, sitting on the edge of the bed.

Death

"Ladi's dead."

It's my friend Deborah on the phone, calling from Evanston, where we grew up together and where she still lives.

In the kitchen of my apartment on the Upper West Side, I hold the receiver away from my ear, as if to distance myself from the message. Ladi. A high school friend—I have a photograph of him in my scrapbook, wearing a beret and my father's bathrobe. We're on our way to a costume party. The year is 1966. Ladi would be my age, fifty-five now—except for him there is no *now*.

"What happened?" I say.

"I don't know. I just heard. I think he dropped dead of a heart attack. He lived two blocks from me, but I hadn't seen him in a few years. I picked up the *Tribune* and there it was . . ." Her voice trails off.

We talk for a while about Ladi, reminiscing. But it's hard. I want to get off the phone and think. Try to put the matter in perspective. To understand what Henry James, in his last hours, called "the Distinguished Thing."

This has been happening a lot lately, I notice. Death—the *fact* of death—has been creeping into my consciousness—subliminally at first, on little cat feet, and then in a torrent of accumulating dread. Twenty-two years ago, when I first came to New York, death was a rare disaster. One friend of mine, Jane, had died of multiple myeloma at the age of twenty-six; I can still see her parents weeping as they sat by the grave-side in a town outside of Boston. For years afterward, I would be walking behind a young dark-haired woman and imagine it was Jane, only to remember with a stab of certainty that it wasn't. But except for the deaths of grandparents—a natural winnowing out of generations—death was a catastrophe; like a plane crash or an accidental drowning, it singled out random victims. I knew empirically that it would eventually happen to me—but not now, not yet. It was a matter that could be post-poned.

People in proximity to my life did die on occasion—a reporter at the *New York Times*, of breast cancer in her mid-thirties; smokers I vaguely knew who got lung cancer. Sometime in the 1980s, my parents' friends began to die, slowly, picked off one by one—not a mass exodus from life, just a thinning of the ranks. An old school friend here, a neighbor there, a guy from my dad's Sunday doubles game. When friends of mine died, it was still a fluke. The ones who did were gener-ally older than I—a lot older. One friend got prostate cancer at seventy-one. I visited him in the hospital a few days before the end. His breath was rasping; he was nearly unconscious. I held his hand. I'd never seen a dying person before who wasn't a grandparent. I was forty years old. Five years later, another friend died of pancreatic cancer. I mourned his loss; I missed him. But he, too, was seventy-one. He had lived his bibli-cal span.

Then something happened. People my own age, or not much older, began to die. I had reached the age where I turned to the obits in the *Times* first—even before the front page. Among the reassuring octoge-

narians and nonagenarians and only slightly less reassuring septuagenarians a headline or photograph would sometimes leap off the page
that squeezed my heart. The *New York Post* executive and man-about-
town Eric Breindel, dead at forty-two. But hadn't Breindel had long-
standing health problems? Mike McAlary, the *Daily News* columnist,
died of colon cancer at the age of forty-one, leaving behind a widow
and four children, one of whom had been conceived after McAlary
learned that he was ill. I read with mounting horror the obit of
Jonathan Kwitny, a journalist who died of a brain tumor at fifty-seven,
leaving behind an infant born six months before he died. Medical
anomalies, I consoled myself. Normal people my age don't die.

Except they do. Death was happening all around me. When I studied the obit pages of my college alumni magazine, there were more and
more entries for people who belonged to the classes of '67, '68, and
beyond. Reading my *Twenty-fifth Anniversary Report,* I learned that
twenty-one of my classmates had died—not that many, in truth, considering the size of my class, nearly a thousand strong. Still . . .

My address book is a necropolis: Allan Bloom, dead. James Breslin,
the Rothko biographer and dear friend, dead. Zita Cogan, friend of Saul
Bellow, dead. And that's just the first three letters of the alphabet.
Neighbors are being carried out of my building at an alarming rate:
Yitzak Rabi, the real estate salesman; Hi Dolinsky, who used to stride
out of the elevator in his tennis whites, racket in hand, and head off to
the Central Park courts every Saturday; the barrel-chested smoker with
the raspy voice whose name I never knew. And it's not just older tenants
who are going: on the evening of 9/11 I get home and Miguel, the doorman, says, "Miss Schwartz, she not here. She work on a high floor."
Clarin, round-faced, funny, who wore 1940s outfits—long skirts, black
stockings, pillbox hats with black lace around the brim. She was stylish,
sexy. I didn't know her well, but we bantered in the elevator. She was a

lawyer in a firm whose offices were on the 106th floor. I try to imagine—I try *not* to imagine—the flames, the conflagration, the fear. Was
she incinerated? Was she one of those who jumped? Clarin. Gone.
Three nights later, when the whole city is supposed to light candles for
those who died in the World Trade Center, I stand in front of our building clutching a candle and watch its flame waver in the dusk.

It's not just the proliferation of the dead that's so unnerving. It's the
sensation, harder and harder to shake off, that whether it happens thirty
years from now or three years from now, it *will* happen. Like a man on a
subway platform awaiting a train whose vibration on the rails prefig-
ures its arrival, I feel its approach. I open up the Sunday *Times* and my
eye falls upon a photograph of a woman I used to know twenty years
ago: I'm stunned to see that she's middle-aged. She looks the same age
my mother looked when I was an adolescent. She *is* the same age. I
study her bony, blue-veined hands with morbid fascination. The photograph of a columnist in one of the tabloids morphs overnight from a
thirtyish woman to a middle-aged matron. How did the editors break it
to her, I wonder, that it was time for a new photograph? At a family
gathering, my cousin Ellen and I gaze at each other sheepishly, embarrassed by what we see: our parents inhabiting our bodies. The transfor-
mation is too abrupt: it doesn't compute. "When I look at myself in the
mirror now," a beautiful fortysomething woman friend of mine
remarks, "I say to myself, 'Who the fuck is that?'" I stand before my own
bedroom mirror in a dark blue suit, eyeing with astonishment a
pouchy-eyed man who looks eerily like me, only much, much older.
This unfamiliar me is middle-aged. *Late* middle-aged.

Death is an inconvenience. We're like the Duc de Guermantes in
Proust's novel, who refuses to acknowledge that a relative is on his
deathbed because it will interfere with a party he wishes to attend.

When informed that the relative has in fact died, the Duc murmurs, "You exaggerate," and goes off to the party.

Not long ago there was an unnerving piece in *Esquire* about the television executive Brandon Tartikoff, who was dying of Hodgkin's disease at the age of forty-seven. The reporter had hung out with him in his last months while Tartikoff answered e-mail and speed-dialed business associates from his hospital bed. He had new shows in development. Two weeks before his death he was still taking meetings. The reporter's last conversation with him was about a battle for control of entertainment programming at ABC. "I don't really care about that story anymore," Tartikoff said in a croaking voice. Two weeks later he was dead. I think of a *New Yorker* cartoon where a receptionist at her desk says over the phone, "He's dead. Would you like his voice mail?"

We're not going gently. We're going the way our generation does everything else. Research it. Make sure you're getting the best deal. Study the alternatives the way we studied alternative families and alternative diets and alternative religions. "Baby Boomers Want Less Pain and More Grace Before That Good Night" reads the headline of a story in the *Times* about scholarly projects in what professionals like to call the "end of life experience." George Soros has given $15 million to a program at Memorial Sloan-Kettering for a study entitled Project Death in America. The Robert Wood Johnson Foundation has allocated $41 million to the problem of how to improve care for the dying. "There is a sea change under way in attitudes toward death," the *Times* quoted Rosemary Gibson, a senior program officer at the Johnson Foundation. "Death is finally coming out of the closet," joked Kathleen M. Foley, chief of pain and palliative care at Memorial. On Sunday nights, we're glued to the set, watching the HBO series *Six Feet Under*.

What to do with the body? Another headline in the *Times:* "More Choose Cremation, Though Cost Can Rival Burial." But that's only if you put the cremated remains in an urn or inter them in a vault. The favored trend—just scattering the "cremains," as they're now called—has a countercultural tinge; conserving land, keeping the funeral simple, disposing of the body in a nonmaterialistic way instead of spending money on a memorial stone harkens back to the less-is-more ethic of the 1960s.

Thomas Lynch, an undertaker in Milford, Michigan, who belongs to the boomer generation, has been publishing funny, lugubrious essays about his business. Lynch, who comes from a family of undertakers, notes that the big players in his line of work are positioning themselves for the baby boom years of reckoning: the next two or three decades, "when the number of annual deaths in the United States will grow by a million compared with today." What are these boomers going to want in the way of a death kit? "Everything is customized," writes Lynch. "The generation now in the market for mortuary wares is redefining death in much the same way that, three decades back, it redefined sex and gender." We're keen on "ecofriendly cyberobsequies," biodegradable coffins, recyclable cremation remains. Eternal peace now.

I have a distinguished friend, Bobby, a specialist in genetics at a leading university, who is doing advanced research on telomeres, the cells that regulate the aging process. He's circumspect about his work, careful to promise nothing, but I know this much: it has to do with finding the switch that turns off the rogue cell. Whenever I see him, I say to myself: *hurry up, Bobby.*

Sometimes I think: What if we're the last generation to die? It amazes me that a normal life span in the Ancient World was thirty; how could they stand it? Future generations will shake their heads in wonder: *Can you believe people used to die? How could they go through life knowing—knowing!—they were going to end up moldering in the earth?* Assuming that I don't get in under the wire—grandfathered in to immortality—I have to make plans. ("Have you secured your plot yet?" asks a well-organized friend as we drive past the cemetery he's chosen in the town where he summers.) Getting into a cemetery is going to be as competitive as getting into private school. Anna is leaning in the direction of the little graveyard in our Vermont town; her father is buried there. It's a beautiful spot, but not that meaningful to me as a final resting place. My parents were supposed to go to Woodlawn Cemetery in Chicago, where their parents are buried, but they sold their plots when they moved away.

One day, trudging up West Seventy-ninth Street behind the Museum of Natural History, I pass the building where Anna and I lived when we first came to New York. I peer into the murky lobby, where a doorman sits on a stool. Albert was the doorman when we lived there, frail and white-haired even then; he would be dead now (unless he was 103). He has been joined in that condition by our landlady, Mrs. Leeder—I know this from our landlady's housekeeper, Ellen, who briefly came to work for us and is also now dead. "This life is like the flight of a sparrow," wrote the Venerable Bede. "From the darkness of a wintry night, it comes into the well-lit space of the mead hall, where you sit at supper, with your companions, with a good fire in your midst, while the storms of rain and snow prevail outside; the sparrow enters, and experiences the warmth and joy and conviviality of that hall; then, just as quickly, he exits through the far window, out into the silent, wintry dark."

Reading the Sunday *Times,* that thick compendium of perishable data, I encounter the testimony of a Wall Street investment banker who declares himself to be on the verge of new challenges. "This is the best time of my life," he says. In some ways, it is. I spend money with less hesitation (it's raining and I can't find a taxi, but a livery car between calls pulls up and offers to take me home for twenty dollars. Fuck it, I say to myself. I'm fifty-five—and get in); I don't care as much what others think of me (I'm at the corner newsstand, unshaven, leafing through a skin mag when Mrs. Gitler, my neighbor in 16D, comes in to buy her *New York Post;* so what?); I sit in the library perusing a fat anthology, *Seven Centuries of English Verse,* and actually enjoy reading Donne's Holy Sonnets ("Death, be not proud") and even understand them, more or less.

But these small pleasures hardly outweigh the draining of the hourglass, the dwindling of time. Wait! What about all the lives I can't live? You mean I'll never make several million dollars in shrewd real estate deals; live on a houseboat in Tiburon, California, and commute to work in San Francisco by ferry; write the great American novel? And what about all the things I've done that I'll never do again? Get stoned at the Newport Folk Festival with the fog rolling in and the crowd standing on chairs screaming for an encore from Bob Dylan; sit on the back porch of a house in Cambridge on a hot summer night and drain a bottle of cheap zinfandel with . . . with . . . with . . . her name will come to me in a minute. Never again to hurtle down Lake Shore Drive at ninety miles an hour in my father's secondhand MG Midget convertible while the sun is coming up over Lake Michigan and I'm on the way home from an all-night party at the apartment of David Lauterstein, whose parents are away in Florida. Only now do I grasp the import of Proust's *memoire involontaire,* the unbidden, thrilling impulse "to secure, to isolate, to immobilize—for a moment brief as a flash of lightning—what normally we never apprehend: a fragment of time in the pure state."

I used to study in a carrel in the basement of my college library that had graffiti etched into the wooden desk. There was one message I would stare at while I was trying to absorb Hobbes's *Leviathan:* "What about death?" Had some bored undergraduate etched this stark question into the scarred wood? Or was it the cynical observation of a jaded professor? Three decades later, the question echoes with a new resonance, shorn of irony. What if death interrupts me before I've finished writing the things I plan to write: the memoir, the essay on biography, the book about Chicago? I'm just beginning to get the hang of things: how to stand up for myself in arguments; how to dress (you don't have to wear a tie to Sunday brunch); how not to lose my temper when a cab-driver takes a wrong turn or my neighbor's dog jumps up and smudges my new khakis with its damp paws; how to meditate; how to be alone; how to accept that I don't like Wagner's operas and never will; above all how to be happy for the simple reason that I'm not dead, have enough money, and no one I love is sick. It took a while, but I almost feel at home. Don't make me check out now!

I'm haunted by the fate of my friend Dave, who finally, after a long lifetime on an academic salary, could afford at seventy to build a library in his country house—the house itself only acquired in his mid-sixties. A month after the architect's plan was approved and the contractor broke ground, Dave was diagnosed with terminal cancer. He was too weak to go up and see the walls rising from the muddy ground, the built-in shelves, the balcony overlooking the verdant fields. By the time it was finished, he was dead.

A year after Dad's death we have an informal ceremony at our house to mark the date. My brother reads from a paper my father had written about the longevity of composers, and my niece, May, reads the opening stanzas of "Sailing to Byzantium," the poem he'd been memorizing at his death. I read a letter, composed in Dad's dry, ironic style, in which he recorded the dialogue of two clerks at his local bookstore who had never heard of the philosopher Jacob Bronowski, one of Dad's heros.

DONALD: Do you have Bronowski's *The Identity of Man*?
CLERK #1 (muttering): Bronowski . . . Bronowski . . . (calls to clerk #2) Hey, Joey! You ever hear of a guy called Bernowski?

CLERK #2: (shaking head): Nah.

DONALD: But he lives right here in town.

CLERK #1 (brightening): Yeah, yeah, yeah. That guy. He comes into the store. (looks up book in card file and says with note of satisfaction): Nope. It's not in stock. Want me to order it?

DONALD (annoyed): Never mind.

CLERK #1: Don't sweat it, Mister. I heard it's not that good.

A couple days later, after everyone has dispersed, I bury Dad.

It's a warm day in late August, and muggy; the sky is overcast. I fetch the urn from the shed, where we put it when Steve brought it up in the trunk of his car. He was relieved: for a year he'd kept it in his closet. ("I was startled every time I opened the door: 'Sorry! I didn't know you were in here.'") The urn is small, a marble beige-and-white-veined vase, but heavy. I embrace it in my arms and go out to the field behind the house that we've chosen as Dad's final resting place. Steve and Mom and I decided this was the best spot, a few yards from an apple tree; we can put a bench under it for when one of us wants to come out and visit him.

I dig. The meadow grass is thick. I dig and dig, tossing shovelfuls of dirt over my shoulder. It's hard work; eventually I hit stones and have to pry them out. I hack away at tree roots. A light misty rain has begun to fall. I pull off my shirt and throw it on the ground, feeling the rain on my naked back.

When the hole is big enough, I embrace the urn again and lower it into the ground. I take the lid off to see Dad one last time, and notice that the ashes are in a plastic bag sealed with a round metal tag. I tear at the plastic and empty the contents of the bag into the urn, scooping up the ash and bone. I pull the tag off and read the words on it: *Mount Auburn Cemetery 55461.*

My heart pulses with alarm: Why Mount Auburn? What if there was a mix-up and this isn't him? *It doesn't matter,* I try to reassure myself.

What difference does it make? But it's bothering me, to the point of panic. *Dad,* I speak to him: *Are you there, Dad? Is that you?* I start to lose it as I crawl around in the dirt, grabbing fistfuls of earth and hurling them into the hole. It's raining harder now, and the dirt is turning to mud. *Dad? Dad?*

Then it occurs to me that the crematorium is at Mount Auburn, and that it's probably him. Calmer now, I continue to dredge up the wet dirt, pushing it into the hole. I'm crawling around on my hands and knees, relieved. I like getting dirty, the feel of the dirt and mud encrusting my skin.

Finally the hole is filled. I pat it down, treading on the grave in my moccasins. We've ordered a stone that we'll put in place next summer, with a simple inscription:

Donald Atlas 1913–2001
"I shall wear the bottoms of my trousers rolled"

The epitaph could be construed as grim—the line that precedes it is "I grow old, I grow old"—but Eliot's *The Love Song of J. Alfred Prufrock* was my father's favorite poem; after much discussion, we agreed that he would have liked it.

I leave a boulder to mark the grave. The stone will be laid into the ground flat so that Ron Pembroke, when he mows the field in the spring, can go right over it.

Acknowledgments

Acknowledgments for long books tend to be long. For this brief book mine are brief. First of all, to my brilliant and exacting editor David Hirshey, who came up with the idea almost before I did—or maybe it *was* before I did—and then saw the manuscript through many drafts. My older brother Steve, who used to twist my arm until I cried "uncle" when we were kids, has twisted it with benevolent intent in this instance— though still not without pain—laboring over each page, each word, and sometimes writing in words of his own. They were so good that I simply transcribed them as they were, so the usual disclaimer that any mistakes are my own doesn't hold in this instance; some of the mistakes might be Steve's. (I forgive him if they are.) Others who pored over the manuscript in a strenuous effort to preserve me from embarrassment were my friends David Boorstin, Dan Menaker, Susan Morrison, Marion Maneker, Deb Garrison, and Jay Parini. Shelly Perron's shrewd and diligent copy-editing saved me from many gaffes, both factual and stylistic. Emily Macdonald gave a late draft fierce scrutiny. Nick Trautwein expertly saw the book through production, adding some good advice along the way. My agents Andrew Wylie and Jeff Posternak are so much more than agents; they, too, are friends who have been advocates of this book from the beginning. And finally, to Anna, without whose love, companionship, and care I might not have survived at all. For me, perhaps more than for most writers, a book is a collaborative effort; for this book in particular, given its sensitive material, I asked a great deal of editorial and emotional support from my early readers, and they—to my deep gratitude—supplied it.